The *Edda* as Key to the Coming Age

# The *Edda* as Key to the Coming Age

## Peryt Shou
### (Albert Christian A. Schultz)

Originally Published 1920

Lodestar
P. O. Box 16
Bastrop, Texas 78602
USA

www.seekthemystery.com

## Acknowledgments

Thanks go to Michael Moynihan for his help in providing copies of originals of the obscure and often difficult figures which accompany this work. An acknowledgment also goes to Manfred Lenz for information he provided concerning the life and activities of Peryt Shou and for information contained on his website:
http://home.t-online.de/home/turbund/prtsh.htm

## Editor's Introduction

Peryt Shou, whose legal name was Albert Christian Georg Schultz, was born the son of an innkeeper on 22 April 1873 in Kröslin near Wolgast in Pommerania. Schultz studied in Berlin and devoted himself to poetry, paining and eventually the secret sciences. During the course of his career he authored some forty books, most of which have been forgotten and lost in obscurity. However, he remains one of the most important esotericists of 20th century Germany. This is mainly because his works, although obscure, were nevertheless extremely influential on other German occultists and esotericists of the day.

Those directly influenced by Peryt Shou include Ludwig Schmitt, Alfred Strauss, G. W. Surya (= Demeter Georgiewitz-Weitzer), Rudolf von Sebottendorf, Hans Sterneder, Arnold Krumm-Heller, A. Frank Glahn, Herbert Fritsche and Karl Spiesberger.

In the early years of Shou's writing and teaching career he concentrated on works relating to the East and to works devoted to a more universalistic view of his major concepts and working theories of cosmic hieroglyphics and "practical Logistics" (*praktische Logistik*). Writing in his *Iatrosophie* (1962, p. 93), Herbert Fritsche (1911-1960) identified these two foundational experiences which awakened Shou to his inner work, i.e " the reading of cosmic hieroglyphics and awakening in the Logos, rebirth in the Word."

By the same token Shou was greatly influenced by the works of Guido von List, as the text of the present work shows. This book, the German title of which is *Die "Edda" als Schlüssel des kommenden Weltalters!*, was the first volume of a series to be entitled *Esoterik der Edda*, published by Linser-Verlag. This volume was first published in 1920. This Armanic influence in the work of Peryt Shou can be most clearly traced from the initial influence of Arnold Krumm-Heller, who published some of Shou's works immediately following the First World War. Throughout the 1920s Shou's work was increasingly under the influence of the growing Ariosophical wave, upon which he conversely exercised his own influence. By the end of the 1920s Shou was in close contact with the leading Ariosophical thinkers, e.g. Rudolf John Gorsleben, Werner von Bülow and Karl Maria Wiligut.

It is interesting to note that Aleister Crowley, while in Berlin showing his paintings, wrote in his diary for February 11, 1932: [Krumm-Heller] here with Peryt Shou.

It appears that Shou lived throughout the National Socialist regime without being molested. This, no doubt, speaks to his good connections. He lived a a private teacher and writer, and continued to fulfill this role after the war.

Shou's work on the *EDDA* is of interest on many counts. It gives a larger context to some of the more difficult sections of the book *Rune Might*, first published in 1989, and recently republished by Rûna-Raven (2004). The whole tenor of Shou's work, although imbued with the general *völkisch* spirit so prevalent in much of German occultism of the 1920s, nevertheless cannot be classified as a work rooted "right-wing" extremism. Clearly Shou's larger sympathies are with universal ideas and patterns, and are not unsympathetic to the idea of "communism"—albeit of a spiritual and not an orthodox Marxist-materialist kind. But just as clearly this work is born of the distressing national circumstances his country found itself in during the years immediately following World War I. It is in this national and historical context that some of the text has to be understood. However, its larger validity can transcend those particular circumstances and related to any and all societies and individuals who find themselves in distress, and who are searching for a way to overcome those difficulties by means of esoteric, spiritual techniques and exercises.

When Shou wrote his book in 1920, Germany seemed as if it had been "crucified" by the events of the "Great War." This feeling must have only increased when, after the country had seemed to be "resurrected" in the Third Reich — as Shou's text seems to foreshadow — it was once more devastated in 1945. When Shou died on 24 October 1953 his country was in fact on the eve of a much more permanent and stable resurrection

Throughout this translation material placed in square brackets [...] are additions or clarifications by the translator. This will often be the provision of the original German word or phrase being translated. The illustrations are exact copies of those which originally appeared in the book

Stephen E. Flowers
Woodharrow
July 23, 2004

# Introduction

The *Edda*,*) as it exists for us today, is regarded as being historically, mythologically, and religiously passé, but not so as to its metaphysical content!

At no time has this ever had as much meaning as it has in the present-day! It is a book of renewal and rebirth, not only for one people but for all of humanity. The Germanic people are, as Gobineau saw, destined for destruction as an independent folk-group, as a race in the old sense.

The *Edda* teaches about the death, the destruction, of the Germanic peoples as a race, the decay of its blood-born divinities; the wolf-age and the Fimbul-age swallow them up! The Germans will be a sacrifice for a new world order, but they — and here the meaning of the *Edda* is fulfilled as a metaphysical, trans-Christian work of poetry — will give life to this order in a particular way.

In the Ninth Night [Hávamál, *Edda***)] Wuotan represents the rebirth of mankind out of a moldering Christianity, and is the inspiration of the world-spirit for the orphaned sons of the Earth— for those whom Nietzsche saw as having been greatly betrayed by Christianity.

Certainly Christianity is something which has evolved historically, and is not something which is spiritually eternal. But according to the metaphysical content of the *Edda* Christ's sacrificial death on the World-Tree was originally the first and final birth of the Germanic God, i.e. his supernatural entry into history!

Wuotan's appearance in the "Ninth Night," his descent from the World-Tree, from crucifixion and death (*Edda*-Hávamál: "Wounded by a spear," like Christ), his re-emergance as Baldur-Wuotan is, seen metaphysically, the great event of our age. In his sacrificial death there is rejuvenation itself!

But only when this sacrificial death is completed will the rejuvenation take place! Only when the Germans die to their age-old demon of race, when they sacrifice the idols of falsely understood Germanism, falsely understood power — and above all the "ego-serving will" — and when they perceive the great struggle of humanity for social self-liberation in the sense of a metaphysical calling, only then will they be resurrected anew and save a mankind, which is now decaying.

---

*) There is an older, so-called *Sæmundar Edda* and *Younger Edda* of Snorri Sturluson. Together they constitute collections of the basic Germanic religious material in poetic and prosaic form.
**) In the present book this is subjected to an exhaustive interpretation. In the same way the most important songs of the *Edda* will be discussed in subsequent Eddic works, especially as regards their esoteric content.

# Prelude

> "It serves no useful purpose to revive a heathen Wuotanism, nor to fight against Christianity, because it has apparently become fruitless of the present day, but rather we should learn to understand *the language so divinity, which speaks in this age more clearly than ever before...*"

The mission of Roman Catholic Christianity ends at the point where Christ died hanging on the cross; however, the mission of Germanic Christianity begins right there: Christ awakening on this World-Tree or cross*) descends alive as Wuotan. Here the secret of the *Edda* is revealed to us as the one and only esoterium**) of humanity. The "High Song" (Háva-mál)***) demonstrates this process.

Figure 1
The awakening on the World-Tree according to the Aryan mysteries of the *Bundehesh*, Wuotan in the Ninth Night ("Hávamál" of the *Edda*— Christ on the cross.

Wuotan awakens on the World-Tree in the "ninth," in the *deepest, night* of humanity by means of a magical runic force— the Need-Rune! Truly no more accurate picture of the present situation could ever be devised. Awaken, you, too, O German spirit, by means of the Need-Rune's force and descend rejuvenated from the cross. Wake up to your hidden regenerative mind as well.

---

*) That "cross" and "world-tree" indicate the same thing in the religious-esoteric conception of the ancients is shown by the following investigations.
**) From Greek *esoteron*, the inner essence as opposed to *exoteron*, the outer essence, especially of religion.
***) In most *Edda*-collections presented as part of "Wodan's Rune-knowledge."

For here no mere poetic or mythological experience is being indicated, but rather a real and, at the same time, deeply religious thing. The descent of Wuotan-Mercurius has to be experienced! He is the only way for the regeneration of humanity, for its Od-ization with spiritual currents, of the saturation of it with a "spiritual element" (Od, thus according to Guido von List and Carl von Reichenbach, "Od-in" = the "Od-awakener"!) after its submergence into matter. The Od-streams, unbound by the Mercurial spirit, "Od-in," save mankind, pulling it upward once more! Whoever is not seized by these Od-streams will go down; the chaotic vortex of matter and the material cosmos will suck him down.

The first phase of Christianity ends with the submergence of humanity in the material vortex, but here at the same moment of general Need,(1) the Mysterium of the "Ninth Night" also goes into action. Nine great lunar cycles have gone by since the death of Christ. Thus, in the Ninth Night, Wuotan loosens himself from the World-Tree, or cross (drasill = gallows, cross), and climbs down, Need calls him. By means of an Odic impulse he becomes the turner of Need as *Deus Odinus*.

The awakening to the Need-Rune, as it is demonstrated in this text, awakens new powers in the human spirit, opens the hidden channel in the heart and voice of the world-spirit as that of a great invisible community of the spirit.

This is what is streaming into our time as the great new experience of a world-wide spiritual context. The Runes are becoming a world-wide language of genius. Thus a new constructive power is rising up to meet the destructive wave of the present-day. A spiritual brotherhood is beginning to unify humanity! With increasing clarity and strength its signals, until now invisible, are working in peoples' souls: The Brotherhood of Hermes is establishing itself on the rubble of Europe as a daughter-colony of a celestial star— as Nostrodamus had already foreseen:

> The long-desired one will never return
> But there appears out of Asia
> One of the Brothers from the Band of Hermes,
> Which unifies all of mankind under it.
>
> [*Centuries* X.75]

The "Hermes-Christians," counted among the oldest Christian communities, developed along a Gnostic-Egyptian lines, in the context of secret cults similar to the mysteries of Hermes-Thoth (Mercurius) among the Egyptians. Here Christ tends to believers of this Earth as the invisible shepherd and king from another star (*"Basileus" tôn ouranôn*).*)

The "High Song" of the *Edda* represents the cosmic mystery of the descent of the Mercurial Spirit (Wuotan = Mercurius according to Tacitus) to the Earth.

Here the Eddic seer is not speaking of mere mystical traditions but rather he is speaking as the mouthpiece of the god himself! He announces his awakening at the time of deepest Need.

---

*) Cf. the texts: *Pistis Sophia* and the *Book of Jeu* from the primitive Christian literature.

The descent of Wuotan from the World-Tree is, as we will presently show, the essence of an old Aryan ritual still to be found in the Zend-scriptures, in the *Puranas* of the Indians and in the *Book of the Dead* of the Egyptians, whose secret, preserved by wise antiquity, must, in a short while, be made the property of the whole world and all of humanity. Otherwise these will be destroyed. So even Christ can not remain what he is—the one on the cross—but rather the time must come when what Gerhard Hauptmann saw will be fulfilled:

> That finally redeemed by the Son's power
> The dead Savior moves his limbs,
> And radiantly, laughingly, full of eternal youth,
> A youth climbs down into the May."

### The New Tree of Life*)
of Humanity (Ygg-drasil) in the Portrayal of the Worker
Gerrit Engelke

I would like to swoop up into thee
  Green Tree.
I would like to surge up —in joyous vigor—
  Into the cells at thy pith
 All the way up into the tree-top dreams
  High above.
I would like to spread out a hundred arms
  Into the breadth of light
  Like branches,
Branching arms with leafy fingers,
  And then to feel, like a flood of light,
  Like the glow of midday,
  Weaving through them.
I would like to soar out of the tree-top
  —Tree of Life—
 Out of the leafy tree
  Like dripping light,
  Like singing wind
  Into cosmic space.

    *Schulter an Schulter* Poems by Workers
    Verlag Vopelius, Jena

---

\*) The problem of "Ygg-drasil," on which the spirit of humanity is rejuvenated — the revived Wuotan according to the *Edda* — is solved here entirely within the meaning of the ancient Aryo-Semitic "Tree of Life," and viewed in exalted poetic vision, in verses of divinatory power. No philological elaboration can describe this phenomenon with equal clarity. We are all growing on invisible etheric trees of an ancient, divinely-originated, culture and race, the branches of which spread out into all peoples. "When its branch becomes succulent and puts on leaves, then ye will know, that the day is neigh."

# Part I

# The Eddic Secret

## 1. The New Experience of God

Christ, the Crucified, led the world to destruction, to death— Christ-Wuotan, the Awakening One on the cross will lead it back to resurrection. Certainly the world had to die, as he did, but it also had to reawaken— as he did, in a higher transformation.

Historicizing dogma could only give us a dead Christ hanging on the cross, the esoteric understanding of Christianity, which is now coming into being, will give us a Christ reviving on the cross.

The Germanic spirit (*Edda* "Hávamál") predicted this long before there was a historical Christianity. Christ, understood purely historically and dogmatically, bids him to be killed a second time. That is what happened. And with him Christianity was killed, slain for "the Lord of this World." The Christian nations had to experience what has happened to them today— death and decay on the cross, they had to enact the drama of Golgotha in its original meaning: to die on its first mission just as Christ did.

But on its second mission the *Edda* sees it once more descending from the World-Tree (cross) called to new life, rejuvenated!

Here the blood — the vibrating crystal within — takes on a certain role! But it should be mentioned that what is "Germanic" in the rebirth is different from what is Germanic in decay and defeat— a drunken self-aggrandizement to some kind of blood-related privileged "caste" among humanity. Even the Botocuds think of themselves as racially superior to all others. Through the divine drop of blood in our veins we are a flock of God. But woe unto those who would make this divine drop of blood bestial, who would blind the visionary crystal — the eye of God — in our veins!

For it is only for the "visionaries" that the new world will shine, not for the "blind," even if they will rule equally for a while! They will die and disappear. The visionaries, however, will remain, for they shall return. The Runic magic of Wuotan, which allows for his resurrection, is a mystery of the blood— but Abraham was also an "Arman"*) (see Tiede: *Urarische Gottes Erkenntnis*) and saw it as well and Jacob too was called by the same thing.

Na-hor, their patriarch is the Egyptian En-her,**) Germanic Einherjar and Char-an, where Jacob was enlightened— a Herian- or Einherjar-place, i.e. a locality of initiation and occult calling over which no earthly legal authority holds sway, only a divine authority!

---

*) Arman, Irmion from Irmin indicates the son of Hermes-Mercury among the Germans, a branch of the Hermes-Brotherhood

**) Already mentioned in the oldest heavenly lists (decan-lists). The name means "turner," the one who tunes in to God, i.e. the ego which recurs in moral rebirth, and which "tunes" the person to God anew.

Every great cultural nation has its calling in blood and spirit, which in all cases exemplifies the modification of the single great secret of the world, and through this modification it establishes its most holy traditions. But we do not know how far each of them has fallen away from, and has ruined, the divine crystal of the blood to the point where it can no longer be recognized.

## 2. Awakening

The descent of Wuotan from the World-Tree (cross), as the great hidden event of our age, takes place by means of a certain inner experience. This text relates to this.

Wuotan is Mercury a spiritual cord waving itself throughout the All. In his recurrence he is no longer a racial spirit in the earlier sense, but rather is a neo-racial being, or universal spirit,*) a shining, blooming spirit of life (Baldur-Beldegg), a renewer of all peoples. Christianity, in its first form, lost its power. "Brotherly love" fell victim to the "power of gold." This is how the *Edda* portrays it.

The Need-ring of the demon (And-vara—Need) burdens mankind as a curse until God comes to redeem man through knowledge of Need.

Wuotan-Christ hangs on the World-Tree (cross), see Fig. 1, dead, unable to move throughout all of the Nine Nights through which humanity has lived thus far, i.e. through the moons of the new birth. In the "Ninth Night" he rouses himself, says the *Edda*— awakening to the Need-Rune and descends from the Tree.

Humanity is supposed to experience this as well. Because the Need, which it is suffering through, is blind and stands under the curse of the demon, of the Eddic "Andvari," and can cause terrible things if it is not struck by a knowledge of the divine, , i.e. if a God does not redeem it! In this sense the Need-Rune shines over the cross of Christ as "INRI," that is, Jesus the "Nazir,"**) the King of the Jews born in the Nazarene city ("Nazareth") who is the King of poverty, misery and the one who overcomes these same things and who was killed for it. It says the same thing as the Need-Rune, on which the dead Wuotan, hanging on the World-Tree, awakens:

| | |
|---|---|
| Nysta ek nidr | Bending myself down, |
| Nam ek upp runar | I took up the runes |
| Aepandi***) nam | Calling Need I took. |

(Wuotan's Rune-Song, as a part of the "High Song")

---

*) O-din relates to Old Norse *odr*-spirit.

*) A "Nazir" is, among the Hebrews, someone who voluntarily suffers Need and thereby mitigates and pays off general Need.

***) From Old Norse *æpa*, to cry out, *æp* a shout of need. Christ died with the words: *ab an'dsawah*, "Father, I commend" [Luke 23.46] which has the same mantic character as the *æpandi*-motif. In Aramaic it is agglutinated.

It should be noted that, the so-called N— Need-Runestave occurs six times here, which for skaldic esotericism is the key to these lines. So Wuotan awakens to the Need-Runes as he bows (*nysta*).(2) Here the ritual of the Ninth Night begins, which is an operation that inaugurates the new experience of divinity.

### III. The Tabernacle of the New Will

If we follow the way of the *Edda* there is one kind of Need that we suffer through blindly and another kind that we suffer through while seeing— this is a divine Need, which leads to salvation. Why doesn't it work in time? Why doesn't this victorious one descend from the cross? The *Edda* gives the answer. Certainly, the one hanging on the World-Tree (cross) will come after the Nine Nights— the nine great cycles of the moon, after nineteen hundred years— that is to say in the present time. He will awaken all peoples to the Need that has gloomily and mortifyingly seized them. He will project his divine, glaring light into the general state of suffering, by means of a holy operation: Bow thee right down Wuotan and "take" those upon the Need-Rune, then within thyself will be ignited the higher Will, the new Will, that shall be born into humanity, that all of a sudden unfolds itself in you and turns the Need: "When ye shall be those who desire with a single Will and when this turning of all Need is also something which is a Necessity [*Notwendigkeit*]."(3)

These words by Nietzsche are actually a call in the direction of the new desire, but they still do not contain the esoterium, for this does not come from the intellect, not from beautiful words, but rather from harmonization with this will itself, from the experience of a communalization, a *communion* with it. Ultimately it is here that all communism finds its fulfillment and salvation, i.e. in communalization with this new will. Ultimately all humanity blends together here, in permanence and solidarity. It causes the new impulse of will to incarnate, it signifies the turning of every Need:

"*O Du mein Wille, Wende aller Not.*" - O, thou, my Will— Turn every Need (Nietzsche)

But this will is not the passionate craving of the masses for whatever sort of material pleasures, but rather it is actually *Will*, and woe to him who does not obey it! Thus the effluence of humanity by the new Will is completed.

Salvation from the gloomy, selfish individual will can only occur in suffering and Need. Humanity is blind until it is vivified in the new Will!

But in its ultimate foundation the *Edda* tells us what this Will is. It is not a blind communistic will-of-the-masses. To serve the heard-instinct is not, as Nietzsche says, an aspiration of the redeemed, higher man.

Wuotan is more then the will of the masses, as Christ is also.

Need is not turned, nor is distress reversed, by submerging oneself in the will of the masses. True communism requires communing, as Nietzsche says, not with the will of the slave, but rather with that of the master, or that of power! In the will itself lies, according to Nietzsche, that which is eternally ascending, the eternally powerful!

But so that this "will to power" does not become an intoxicating, tyrannical or dictatorial will, nor a mere "idea," in which form it could be even more dangerous, but rather so that this Will functions in a wholesome manner—it is indeed that which we are presenting in this work—, i.e. the cultural bond, the movement of spirits upward, this is the prototypical language of a cosmic community of all conscious beings.*) Because Will is not merely craving, desire, but rather it is a constructive power in the universe (see Schopenhauer, *The World as Will and Imagination*), it functions in a god-like fashion and God is at the same time an epithet of this great spirit-community's willfulness.

In a secret prototypical language, in its "runes," this cosmic-will speaks in an ascending way out of Need and death and mire— as it is stronger than anything else for the one who knows these signs, and who stands there in the tabernacle of the new Will.

### IV. Essence of the Eddic Idea of God

Everything godlike is something which is telepathically spiritual. Within us there is an unfolded antenna**)-cross, the cross of Christ, on which we hang as if dead, because we do not answer to the one universal spiritual wavelength. But whenever we awaken on this cross, then we come to understand the language of the one spirit! Dead, the person hangs on this cross like Christ and Wuotan, but the Ninth Night draws near, in which he shall awaken.

It is the technique itself, which approaching divine knowledge, conveys the secret, the spirit submerged in nature, which becomes free and breathes upward toward the universal spirit.

Lucifer's deliverance!

Nature is divine! Happy that we live in it and not in that laboriously constructed "paradise" the church promises us and which is supposed to await us after death.

But rather paradise is here and now if we know the harp of the forces of nature, and have the plectrum to strum it with— if in the "Ninth Night" we correctly understand that fundamental Rune-force in which the World-Tree itself, roaring and trembling, casts the god down.

It is this which the *Edda* has transmitted to us in its "High Song."(4) O god dissolve yourself, you builder of all things from the beginning, you wise technician and engineer, who has also unfolded us onto a fine remote controlled network of the most sensitive currents.

Teach us to deploy this network as well, just as Jesus taught his disciples, "to cast the net·in the perceptual space (hand) of their physical vehicles (ships)." John 21.6.

---

*) The skald or Arman has an insight into this runic being, he is absolutely the only man enlightened by Wuotan's single-eye (*sahasvara*, pineal gland). Not the sensory eyes, but rather only the spiritual eye opens it up. The "runes" are the script of the "gods," in which they speak, i.e. high beings out of the entire solar realm, and even from the realm of the whole universe, who make use of the telepathic power of the Runes.

**) Antennas are the broadcasting and receiving wires of radio telegraphy which are also stretched out in the form of a cross.

For by doing this they perceived the language of the one Christ
resounding through everything, who from planet to planet, i.e. in
"heaven," weaves the one spiritual band.

Truly, the only hell is this earth, which does not dance the roundelay
of the heavenly sisters, held down by Saturn's dark crown, which
deceives itself by believing that bestial lust is the blessedness of faith,
seduced and confused, which remains ignorant in emotional Christian
indecision and indifference, unable to rise up from the dark matrimonial
bed which they fell into.

Teach us to spread out the tabernacle in which your currents
circulate, all-loving genius of the world, as Israel at one time knew about
the language which resounds in your tabernacle.*)

But delusions of power whips up a brain which has lost awareness of
God, a tower which never comes to a point, like the one in Babylon,
which is broken by the storm of God.

Build a Jacob's Ladder, do not build a tower of power, for you have
confused the languages of the nations with this tower.

The ruler will be ruled, but the servant will be served— by the angels
on high.

The servant will rise, yet the mighty will fall.

"I serve" is greater than "I rule," yet the greatest of all is "I rule in
that I serve," for this rulership will be eternal!

Here the tent of the "Ninth Night" is opened! The circulating
currents from above obey this sound: "I serve." These currents are the
licking waves, the "tongues," which also spoke hovering above the first
Christians.

A radio impulse from above awakens the resounding network within.
World-wide Pentecost.

A wave of magical power links up the spirits of individuals and
allows them to understand one another again as upon that first Pentecost
(Acts 2). That which destroys the "tower" restores the "tabernacle," the
tabernacle of silence, the quietude in God, the tabernacle of conception.

And out of the deep silence the god lifts up his clarion cry, his cry of
need, the first sad outburst of the soul in a voice calling from far away.

It resounds, it arises out of the chaos with the sound of a golden light
with a new creative cry: "Let there be."

It casts the new anchor of light (Fig. 9) into the individual linked to
its ray, it makes him into a member of the spiritual world, that
everlastingly populates the universe.

This is the esoterium of the "Ninth Night."

---

*) In the tent of revelation.

# V. The Ninth Night

Wuotan is one of those enlightened beings of antiquity, the *manusis*, about which the Indo-Aryan *Puranas* speak, and which were later elevated to "gods."

He is an emissary from above, he comes from the realm of light. Great are the worlds up there and neither limited by the withered earth-bound human senses, nor by professional conceit nor even by the sophistic spirit of humanity. Whoever wishes to know them has to learn to bow down, to release himself into the breath of light, and hang himself on the World-Tree for the Nine Nights, he must experience that which the *Edda* wants him to experience. It is no book for the soul of philological shopkeepers and killers of the spirit, but rather it is one for living spirits which ignites the works of Wuotan. Death on the cross, or World-Tree, is transformed into a "descent of the spirit into matter!" The *Edda* shows us that nameless need we are suffering through today and through which we have suffered. The painful Ninth Night came over humanity: "Wuotan-Christ dead on the World-Tree ("Song of the High One," Hávamál)! No salvation for mankind! Hate, baseness, mockery of Hell— *Bestia triumphans*!

What good is Christianity if its greatness is not allowed to breathe freely, and does not transform its exoteric*) crucifixion into an esoteric**) awakening? Was not Christianity intended to be more? We assert that it can no longer exist in the Roman Catholic spirit. We respect the deeply ardent, intoxicating mysterium of genuine old Catholicism— as long as it was taking care of its task—expanding the mystery of the passion of Christ and deepening the raw customs of occidental paganism in the people's souls by transforming them into a patient devotion to God. Thus Novalis was able to say: "The old Catholic faith was an applied, living Christianity. Its omnipresence in life, its love of art, its deep humanity, its joy in humility, obedience and loyalty, make it unmistakable as a true religion."[*Die Christenheit oder Europa: Ein Fragment* (1799)]

But a new breath entered mankind which the church no longer understood.

In the mere imitation and reenactment of the passion of the Savior humanity lost its best qualities, the "marrow in its bones," as Nietzsche reprimands: Humanity being deprived of its soul rather than strengthening its soul! The reason for this was that the will that guided Christianity broke up into two aspects: dogma and original teachings. Christians began to browbeat instead of liberate, to enslave rather than serve, as Christ had intended.

The Church lost its "divine inspiration" because it lost its power over its souls, that redeeming, forceful bond with them, which is "I serve." The illuminating force of this phrase, the empowerment toward leadership of humanity which is sealed within it, was extinguished. The will to power, the will to rule, was the decisive moment. But here the saying: "They should have let the word stand" is fitting.

---

*) Exoteric, i.e. relating to the outer spirit of religion.
**) Esoteric, i.e. relating to the inner spirit of religion.

The Germanic soul began to ignite itself in the evangelium anew, the work of clarification by the great "purifier" commenced. Christian mystics: Angelius Silesius, Tauler, Suso, Eckhart, Jakob Böhme took up the spark, Schelling, Hegel, Fichte fashioned out of it the German self and as Houston Stuart Chamberlain notes, in Kant Protestantism puts forth its nationalistic reblossoming, only then to fall flat once more in learned biblical criticism.

The Great War ignited ancestral memories in the German folk. Wuotan was once more before their gaze, suffering, hanging on the World-Tree, unredeemed, dead. (Figure 1.)

German folk, know here, where your mission begins! Is your soul not crucified like Wuotan? Are you not starving in these bloody, deep, dark Nine Nights, such that the Need-magic, the power of the Need-Rune, ought to redeem you?:

| | |
|---|---|
| Neigend mich nieder, | Bowing down, |
| Nahm ich auf die Runen | I took up the runes |
| im "Notschrei" (*æpandi*) | in a cry of Need |

"Hávamál" (*Edda*)

The fact that the stave of the N- or Need-Rune has been repeated six times here has already been noted above. "Ye doubters, I heard your 'cry of Need,'" Zarathustra said turning to the eagle (Germany) and Nietzsche's *Zarathustra* concludes with the "great cry of Need" and with the "sign."

In the ancient mysteries the "mystical cry of redemption" serves as a sign of the *katochê* (possession) or affiliation of natural thought in the one possessed (*katochumen*) or the one to be initiated. Whether it is the *iakchê* of the Eleusian mysteries or the *Evoe* of the Bacchanalia, the *Onre* (*Onover*) of the rites of Osiris, the INRI of the primitive Christians, it is always the "Rune," i.e. "the inner power of a whispering holy word," which strikes redeemingly like a bolt of lightning into the soul and liberates its potency.

Wuotan, the "Enlightened One," proclaims to his skalds: "Behold, I hang on the World-Tree, dead, for nine nights unredeemed, wounded by the spear"— here one is reminded of the piercing with the lance of the centurion (John 19:34). "They offered me neither bread nor wine" (Hávamál), i.e. no holy communion could redeem Christ from the cross of death any more. He was dead and empty. Then the magic of a Rune and the power of redemption began to work: "*Æpandi nam*" in the original text. Thus we approach the Rune-magic (*runar-galdr*) of Wuotan:

| | |
|---|---|
| Veit ek at ek hekk | "I know that I hung |
| vindga methi á | on a windy tree |
| nœtr allar níu | nine long nights, |
| geiri undathr | wounded by the spear |
| ok gefinn Othni | consecrated to Odhin |
| sjálfr sjálfum mér | I myself consecrated to myself."(5) |

## VI. Wuotan— the Prehistoric Christ of the Germanic Folk!

Perceiving the secret of the Need-Rune Wuotan-Christ descends from the World-Tree (cross).

Does not the Need-Rune shine, as we saw, over the head of Christ as INRI? The *N* in this word is interpreted as "Nazarenus," Hebrew *nazir*, i.e. someone "who suffers distress (need) voluntarily." Nazareth was a "place of nazarenes" in Galilee situated on the western slope of the Tabor not far from Endor, famous for the enlightened woman of Endor, who was by no means a mere sorceress, otherwise we would not have been able to conjure the exalted spirit of Samuel (I Samuel 28:7). She was much more of a true Albruna among the Galileans— a wise and initiated woman. A Nazarene is one who abstains, who voluntarily takes Need upon himself in order to, as the skalds also taught, be redeemed by "Need-magic." Here Need is not merely generalized suffering, but rather, as Guido von List rightly interprets it: The compulsion of fate and the recognition of this (*karma*). It is also the secret of Wuotan's birth according to the *Edda*. In other words: The German God Wuotan-Christ appears to his folk at a very specific cosmic moment.

The descent of Wuotan from the World-Tree (cross) refers to something that is, and will be! At the moment when Need-magic is fulfilled in the German people, Christ, the dead Christ, is transformed on the cross into the descending Wuotan of the Hávamál.

It is completely erroneous to see a heathen ideology of a purely mythological nature in the Aryan wisdom of the *Edda*. Of course, the outward appearances are drawn from that time, just as when Jesus speaks of vineyards, winepresses and the casting out of devils, which are no longer a part of current thinking, the kernel of these representations is nevertheless conceptualized in a timeless fashion— *sub specie aeternitatis*. The images and wonders of the *Edda* speak as much to the eternal things as do those of the New Testament!

For this reason it can also not be said exactly when in time the descent of Wuotan*) from the World-Tree occurred. Actually, it does not exist in time, but rather it is attached to an eternal law in the history of human evolution.

As Gobineau eloquently expresses it: The Germanic race will be the sacrifice for the rest, precisely because it is, in his opinion, the highest! But is this sacrifice necessarily death? Is not the death of Christ really much more only his birth?

Doesn't Wuotan's being sacrificed (Eddic *gefinn*) on the World-Tree mean the same thing? Cannot the power of the Germanic peoples be installed in a manner very different from how we usually imagine it today, different from that which the human mind can even conceive?

---

*) Wuotan, Gwode (oldest name) is, as Logos, the equivalent of the biblical *k'wod*, *kewod*, the future appearance of Christ in Glory or Transfiguration in the Flesh.

It is much more correct to preserve for the divine will in history trust, devotion and loyal service — that most noble Germanic characteristic — and to believe in the one who as Wuotan-Christ brings forth the Need-magic! We repeatedly come back to this one point in the "High Song" of the Germans! Lamenting, suffering, unredeemed, hanging on the World-Tree (cross) the god awakens to a new life. Redeemed by a cry! of what sort it this cry? A cry of lament says the *Edda*. Once this cry has sounded, then it is said in the "High Song" that: From the word a word a word is evolved," which is reminiscent of the doctrine of the Logos in the Gospel of John. Primeval wisdom is revealed from one Rune, a hieroglyph of the World-Tree, to the next. The signs of heaven assume power! They fall to the Earth!

When he comes "the stars will fall to the Earth" [Rev. 8.10; 9.1] Christ says. Are these really the stars? Is it not much more the secret regulating forces of them sealed by the power of God? They fall to earth, regulate, punish and comfort humanity, all unsealed by a force of Rune-magic, by the Rune of the "compulsion of fate," of *Need*. *Karma* will judge humanity through the hieroglyph of the celestial Wold-Tree. We come ever closer to the one great secret. The power of the compulsion of fate, of *karma*, which holds our folk captive, delivers us unto our enemies, and vanishes in an instant when we become aware of it, when we recognize it!

A mystery underlies every compulsion of fate. It is not inflicted blindly, not a punishment delivered by the hand of man or god, but rather such a compulsion of fate is a procreative mystery! In it unfolds the loving fervor of God, of Wuotan, brought forth in pain. But such pain is an excruciating desire under the control of a procreative God— the deepest rapture— as Nietzsche says: We should become those who procreate, and bring things forth! For this reason in the old Germanic magic the N-rune (the so-called Nôt-Rune) was written on the fingernail of the index finger(6) as a reenactment of Wotan's deed of salvation, of perception of the sweet procreative mystery of God. Also medieval German painters show Christ judging with the "Need-finger," awakened to life in the Ninth Night, i.e. reigning over the nine spheres.*)

In reality Armanic knowledge lies behind all this— transcending the Christian horizon. But innate in it all is that experience of God which procreativity flows through the body with the force of the Need-Rune and awakens a divine primeval knowledge within:

| | |
|---|---|
| Fimbul-ljód níu | Nine main-songs I heard |
| nam ek af inum froda syni | from the highly wise son |
| Bölthornis Bestlu födur | of Base-thorn, the father of Bestla |
| ok ek drykk of gat | then I got a drink |
| ins dyra mjadar | of the choice wine, |
| aüsinn Ódrœri | made from Ód-rœrir's foam. |
| thá nam ek frævaz | Then I began to grow |
| ok fródr vera | and be wise, |
| ok vaxa ok vel hafaz | And I seemed refreshed in vigor.(7) |

---

*) In the *Edda* therese are called the "nine mothers" on the edge of the world, i.e. forming the spheres of the world.

Here we discover the process of the divine birth of Wuotan. He sank down as the son of light, as an emissary from above, into the material womb of the earth, of the nine spheres, i.e. into the spiritual essence of our planet. Like Heimdall, who is only the Wuotan of another Germanic tribe, he is conceived by "nine mothers"— the maternally procreative forces of the earth. (See Fig. 1) Here he finds wisdom already prefigured, nine *logoi* or head wise-ones; he learns them from the son of Base-Thorn (Böl-thorn)! Christ, having descended into the earth-spirit, had already saturated the spheres with his spiritual essence, he had already become the earth-spirit, when Wuotan sank down.

By the name "Böl-thorn" is meant the one who is born of the mystery of the "Sin-ai" in the glowing thorn-bush, i.e. Jehovah, whose son Christ calls himself. Thus we discover who this son of Böl-Thorn is. That burning bush is no ordinary thorn-bush, but rather it is the "Protector of Primeval Knowledge," the sleep-thorn of the *Edda* (hedge-thorn), which here once more flares up, and again reveals its secret which had been concealed by Wuotan himself. It burns once more ignited in the spirit of Moses and enlightens him through its sign!

Thus the ancient Aryan theosophy is replicated here. The thorn-bush of the "Shin-ai" (= "place of the thorn") is the sacred Thorn-Rune (Fig. 3b) of the son (Thor) in ancient Germanic theology. Thor, who dwells in the reddish element, in fire, is signified by the Thor- or Thorn-Rune. This is Thor (i.e. the Thunder-Word Logos), who is also Jehovah-Adonai, who appeared before Moses.

The call of God drove Moses up the holy mountain and there had him find the magical Need-Fire, through which he shows the way to salvation for his people.

The initiation of the *Armanen* ensues from the Need-fire and the Need-water. Wuotan, taking up the lament — and Need-Rune — from the earth, awakens and falls down to earth. He is redeemed, God, by means of a magic— Need-magic! He is generatively inflamed by the force of a Rune, of the first ones he takes up — *œpandi*\*)— the Rune of the cry of distress. "Verily ye strange ones I have heard your cry of distress!"

The meaning of sacrifice, which gives all that is divine its life, is made perfect. Divinity is sacrifice! If life is to be brilliantly illuminated by the Eternal, the flame of sacrifice must be ignited within it— a flame that burns in the Need-Rune, and is the hidden meaning of that Rune, and for this reason God awakens upon it.

He who shines in continuous self-conflagration, the solar-spirit Christ who is enlightening humanity, descends from the cross once more living— awakened by the magical power of a Rune! No longer is he the dead man on the wooden cross. He is the divine, who is eternally in his sacrifice — in all that is earthly, in all that is transitory, so that he consecrates and transfigures everything with his sacrifice. He transfigures Need, apparent privations in the material plane, abstinence and suffering into joyous procreation and regeneration! Flowing with a force of the magical Rune throughout the body of the suffering one, he, God, suddenly becomes human, canceling out all distress.

---

\*) From *öp*, Old Norse for "cry of distress, pain."

The meaning of this "High Song" must be fulfilled!

Distress will, and has to, force us to our knees, until we complete the sacrifice, that we might redeem God himself! For this reason Wagner even has his *Nibelung*-drama conclude with the call: "Salvation for the Savior!"(8) This is the meaning of the Eddic poetry which finds its ethically highest expression here in the Hávamál.

## VII. Salvation for the Savior

> . . . until finally saved
> by the power of the son. . .

Christ-Wuotan is a Solar Being! He shines and shimmers in the every-day image of light, but humanity, in its craze for power and erroneous beliefs, has alienated itself from him, and has destroyed and killed the light. If Christ is seen as dead on the wooden cross, so too is his breath extinguished among humanity! He no longer inspires anyone with the spirit of his daily light. For this reason it is said (Daniel 8:11, etc.) that the "daily sacrifice," the sacrifice of the day will someday be abolished. We have fallen into materialism.

St. Francis of Assisi saw Christ crucified in the midst of the sun, and this is the way painters in the Renaissance portrayed him. He saw him as a crucified Solar-Being!

The sun lights, "enlightens," the world by burning daily— thus say our chemists— but as it burns it provides life and energy to all beings and is the fundamental precondition for their existences.

When the fathers of humanity, the *pitres* of the *Veda*, recognized this, they created the sacrifice— the solar sacrifice upon which even today the Brahmanic ritual is based.*) They gazed more simply and more naturally into the world and saw the *truth*. They saw the being which constantly renewed itself in daily self-combustion as a God of Light, which sacrificially pours itself into the world and thereby creates life— continuous life! They saw with sacrificially conditioned senses! For when they recognized the secret of the great constellation, they *sacrificed*! They did what the "inexorable solar will" (Nietzsche) demanded of them, and they remained with this solar will!

But when Vogt, Moleschott and Büchner(9) came and elevated carbon and nitrogen to the level of the solar soul, that "daily sacrifice" ceased. Intellectual hubris and megalomania set themselves on the throne of the archangels and preached the removal of the soul from the world.

Now Christ was really dead— and thank goodness, they slew him a second time, as Cain did Abel, the Apollonian solar spirit!

Thereupon distress came over a now starving and dispirited mankind which had ceased the "daily sacrifice." It had to come. What could be more necessary for mankind? Then came "Need-Knowledge." As enlightenment it fell like a ray of the new Christ-essence— first into the hearts of men, but a flame was soon ignited in them.

Awakening to the "Need-knowledge" the Aryan solar-spirit, Wuotan, arose from the World-Tree (cross). A new impulse originated at that moment— a longing for the visionary solar-sacrifice!

---

*) See *Heilkraft des Logos* by the author.

The descent of Wuotan from the World-Tree constitutes an old Aryan ritual. According to the *Bundehsh* when the Zaotar of the Parses performs the solar sacrifice before the holy tree and speaks the word of salvation, here too divinity descends and reveals itself in the celebrant.

The tree of eternal life and eternal rejuvenation (*ez ha-hajim*) in the Bible is the heavenly tree of the Aryo-Germanics. Only the gods (*elohim*) eat of its fruit and live by it eternally. Therefore even Jehovah says: "'Adam is become as one of us.' So that he might not eat of the fruit of the *ez ha-hajim* and live eternally [God] drove him out of paradise. . ." [Genesis 4.22-23] The passage sounds like the creator is jealous of his creation!

The "fruit of the Tree of Life," of which the gnostic eats and thereby lives eternally and continually rejuvenates himself, is Od. Whoever knows the Od-law and preserves it, finds in it the key of eternal youth in the flesh.

Guido von List explains "Od-in" as "Od-in(side)." Linguistically in Old Norse Od*) signifies the substantial spirit as opposed to the abstract one. In other words this is the spiritual essence, the indivisible bond of spirit and matter, which actually signifies the Od in the way it was meant in the original language.

This Od is found in the world of appearances only in its polarized form, but as it divides, it loses its higher quality, its spiritual-divine vibratory energy. But Od-in tries to preserve just this quality, and for this reason he is called "Od-in(side)," or "Od-(with)in."

The descent of Odin from the World-Tree is the secret of the Od-ization of the ego! The material substance of the ego is transformed into a more materially refined Odic one by the energy of this ritual. It is the same material of the body, but it takes on another vibrational form, one in which it becomes obedient and subservient to the Logos, whereas the natural, material body is instinctually fettered by sin. Thus, only through "Need" is the transformation effected— awakening to Od-in. The sinful flesh will not voluntarily resolve into the spiritually divine or Odic corporeality.

A brass ring encircles the material, and therefore the carnal, atom— the "Need-Ring" (*Andvara*(10)-*nôt*), which the atomic spirit, the material spirit (i.e. the dwarf Andvari) guards. This material spirit within must be conquered, and this is not accomplished easily. Every sin against the flesh must be cleared away. Not only the individual, but he whole of humanity as well, goes through Need until it is converted into an Odic, spiritually divine, essence— completed as Od-in. This is the descent of Od-in into humanity. This Od-in is Christ in the (Od-)cloud. The material body can not receive Christ, only the Odic one can do this! The Od-shell around the body is the cloud in which Christ will once more appear (Matthew 24:30).

Fundamentalist Christians want to see this "cloud" as a vaporous formation in the aether and endow the whole process with a staging they think "worthy of the subject." The real Christian knows that the kingdom of heaven does not *come through outward gestures*, but rather may only be expected inwardly!

---

*) According to Moebius the Od-animus ratio.

The "odic cloud" surrounding a person, the so-called "aura," possesses the image of heaven, a stratification according to the order of the spheres. This is even how modern metaphysicians (Marques, Baraduc cf. Feerhow *Die Aura*) represent it.

Christ frees himself from the World-Cross up above as Od-in, surrounded by an Od-shell.

This liberation is the secret of the Ninth Night (see the next chapter). It results from the energy of the Need-Rune, whose seal must be broken and whose secret must be recognized. The return of mankind to a divine state proceeds through Need. All sins against the flesh have to be, as we showed, canceled out according to a higher "Necessity," according to *karma*! Only then will there be a resolution of the corporeal materiality of humanity into the Odic, divine— into that which is eternally youthful. Thus we see why Od-in broods lamentingly over the Need-Rune until he falls down from the tree. Aren't we experiencing this today— the struggle of the Aryan spirit over Need and Death?

According to the *Edda* Od-in is also bound by the Need-Ring of Andvari— the Ring of the Law and Spirit of Matter. So the dwarf*) (Andvari) rages in the present age of humanity, hindering the penetration of light into our world, as the ring continues to burden the hearts of men terribly. Its curse can only be broken one way— when sin is voluntarily canceled out and taken upon one's self, when the heart bows down humbly even to the blows of God. For the expiation of one's own guilt and shortcomings gives miraculous, and the sweetest, knowledge, growth, and singular progress to the soul. For the humble person divinity breathes sweetness into his suffering, but it destroys the arrogant person.

There is no dogma about how this energy and truth are received by the person through the voluntary expiation of his own guilt. For this reason too we see why the Need-Rune is the same as INRI, i.e. "Jesus, who is a Nazir, he is the King of the Jews." He will be known as a king of humanity! But as he broods over the Nazarene secret, he will descend as another, as one transformed in the Ninth Night!

---

*) A dwarf because he is infinitely small hidden within the atom,

## Part II
### Practical Esotericism of the *Edda*

---

## I. The Secret of the Ninth Night
The solar wheel or swastika is the primeval Aryan sign of salvation:

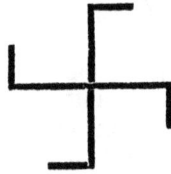

Figure 2

whose secret in the ancient solar rites has a great meaning. When this wheel was rotated*) around a half-axis, i.e. in the angle of the Need-Rune:

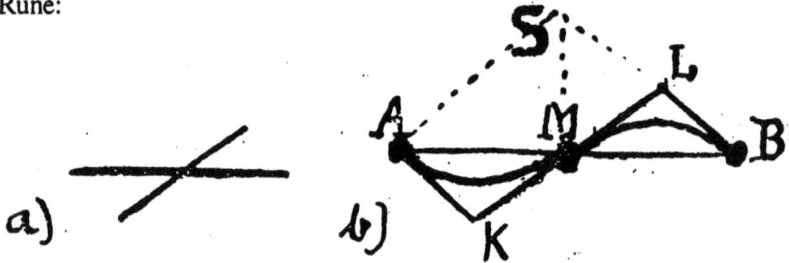

Figure 3

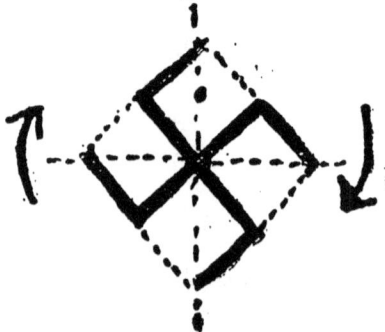

Figure 4

---

*) This rotation occurs in that, as is demonstrated here, the Need-Rune is caused to vibrate in the *hands and hips*, i.e. in two main centers of the body— an Od-positive and an Od-negative one. If the current between the two is closed, as is shown here, when the hands are placed on the hips, then the great *chakram* in the chest (M) is engaged in vibratory motion. It becomes active and so the solar wheel, whose energy it embodies, also achieves an active condition.

Thus appears the High-Need-Sign of the Kaland-brotherhoods*), the seal of the "secret tribunal"!

It is the sign of the Sons of Mercury (Odin *id est* "Deus Mercurius") which opens the sluices of their spiritually divine energy, and they respond to these with knowledge of Ygg-drasil**) with energy streams.

For this is the esoterium of Wuotan. It is none other than the *Intelligentsia Mercurii*, and interplanetary radio network broadcasting to us from the planet Mercury.

"Gods" (Old Norse *regin*)***) are the communicative channels between and among the "children of the sun," the planets!

Venus embraces us with Vanic currents. Her electro-magnetic potential (*"albedo"*) chiefly promotes the function of the internal glands, along with the secretional activity and elevation of the emotional curve resulting from this activity, from the pineal gland (artistic vision) to the genital glands (love)†)

Mercury is the planet of innervation, for which modern science has established absolute mathematical laws,††) which are the same on Mercury as on Earth.

There is only one form of mathematics in the entire cosmos.†††) Mercury is the planet of this immutable adherence to law and of the "wheel,"◊) that vibrates to the rhythm of this law.

It transfers thought-waves from one planet to another. Whoever understands how to "turn" it possesses the secret of the "Brothers of Hermes,"◊◊) *Ygg-dra-sil*, of the world-cross (*drasil*-cross, gallows) and of the World-Tree!

Wuotan descended from it, he who knows about the law of of *drasil* (generation of salvation through turning, see above).

He taught those moved by him, for whom he ignited the single eye—the spiritual eye—how to turn the wheel. And when they turned it—through the Need-Rune (see Fig. 3)—the divine son of Mercury descended.

---

*) Brotherhoods of Hermes, among the Germans called *Irmionen* or *Herminionen*.

**) I.e. according to von List: the "ego" (**ig**) creates— by means of turning (**dra**)— salvation (**sil**).

***) The basic stem is related to setting right or installing something, in this case, cosmic currents.(11)

†) Venus is therefore the planet of love and of "artistic vision."

††) Cf. the discoveries of Helmholtz, Hering, et al.

†††) According to Galileo the book of the cosmos is written in mathematical symbols.

◊) Rota of Enoch in the Kabbalah. By means of turning the wheel Enoch overcame death and is the first to step beyond without dying.

◊◊) Hermes, the Mercury of the Greeks.

Wuotan is not a single entity in the human sense, but rather he is the community of the Hermes-Brothers, who bear the concealed name: "League of Truth." (In this name the movement of the wheel occurs. See the ritual, chapter 6). The wheel of necessity, however, sealed by the so-called *Anda-* or *Need-Rune* — which Theosophy calls the "wheel of karma and rebirth"— is the key to all solar mysteries, great and small. In his informative book, *Uranische Gottes-Erkenntnis* (Herm. Barsdorf-Verlag, Berlin) Ernst Tiede demonstrates the derivation of all the runic symbols from the "rotated swastika," the holy eight-fold star of the solar god (Is-phar, Sa-phir).*)

This star is Mercury, *Asboga*, i.e. the Eight-fold one, which is also named in the Kabbalah. The Secret Eight,(12) the sign of the great concealed Court of God is symbolized by this star. This tribunal is still exercised by an elect troop of the Hermes-Brotherhood*) who have their point of origin in the North.

The Mysteries of Mercury existed in our race from the beginning. The Wolves of the Sun (cf. the essay by Heyse-Zürich in *Psyche*)**) constitute a priesthood on Mercury which is hostile to Wuotan and to whom he succumbed (this Wuotan is said to be consumed by the wolf), but by the power of his higher knowledge he is able to achieve resurrection again. A reflection of this event is found in the death and resurrection of Christ on earth.

In the mysteries of the Greeks the same story of the overthrow and eventual victory of the sons of Hermes is told.

The solar-wolf, Saturn, the "swallower," is here overcome by the higher intelligence of Zeus!

The "veiled stone" which serves the son of Rhea***) in sparing him from the maul of the "sun-wolf," the "swallower of his children," is the holy gleaming jewel whose brilliance none can withstand and which is the key to Greek eschatology— the eight-fold crystal or star of the eternal mysteries!

Thus Clemens the Egyptian says in his *Stromata*: "Whomsoever Christ reawakens to life, shall be transported to the Octad!"

In a contemporary German film a Nordic Frouwa is enthroned as "The Ruler of the World" [*Die Herrin der Welt*] in front of the eight-fold solar disk:

Figure 5
The eight-fold solar disk of the Ophirites according to the film
*Die Herrin der Welt* by Figdor(13)

---

*) Kabbalistically generated by *temurah* (vocalic re-arrangement) of Is-phar or ha-Is-phar (Ahasverus = the one in all, who eternally transforms, and who is therefore the eternal wanderer.
**) Rhea-Cybele is the mother of the Cabeiri, the "eight gods" which again points back to Mercury. The son of Rhea is Zeus.
**) Vol. I, numbers 8-10.

The pose shown in Figure 5 is also sacral and corresponds to the "protector of Yggdrasil" or of the Tree of Life even among the ancient Persians and Babylonians, Figure 6:

Figure 6

This protector is shown here speaking the holy word of enchantment and liberation from the tree of heaven beneath the eight-fold star.

Through the magical power of a sacred gesture the solar word liberates and, in a living way circulates through, the body and thus unbinds from the wooden cross the one who is "crying out in Need." He is the law of the antenna that in a certain direction and longitude provides evidence of the "modulation" toward the spiritual broadcaster, and responds to him.

In the atmosphere there are also "sending"-waves or "*sint*"-waves*) of this kind, in which the spiritual impulse of our faraway brothers in the solar realm vibrate. These can be "tuned into," and then one can come under the protection of invisible spiritual entities.

In reality there is only one spiritual wave that functions throughout the whole system and by which all spiritual beings are bound together.

Thus it was the work of religious consecrations and exercises to make men aware of the real interconnectedness of all spirits. There was no death for the one touched by this wave! Neither would any individual being die out in this whole wave-system (Eddic *Eli-vag*). Moreover there was a constantly renewed sprouting forth on the invisible spiritual tree, the Ygg-dra-sil, in a recurrent springtime of life (Nanna and Baldur-mysteries). Just as the bloom on a tree is always renewed after the course of its given lifetime, and in it the "soul of the tree" appears once more, producing a seminal fruit containing its own image, so too does the "I" always bloom forth renewed on the divine Tree of Life.

---

*) The name of the *sint*-waves (cf. the German word *Sintflut*, "deluge, flood") originates in the scholastic learning of the Middle Ages. The *Sint*- or *Chent*- waves indicate the astral light. Cf. the lists of the decans in the writings of Firmicus Maternus, who was much read in the Middle Ages.

In this sense Wuotan also hangs on the Tree of Life in the cosmos, a reflection of the "I," that patiently awaits his own awakening, a link in the great spiritual chain that extends throughout the universe, and which constitutes the true secret of the "Kingdom of Heaven," the *Basileia tôn ouranôn*. In all the heavens, in all spheres of creation there is one realm of spirits—of spiritual entities—and all are connected by the One over which, according to the *Edda*, Wuotan lamentingly broods until everything is unsealed to him and he descends. Is it not so that this seal is impressed on the heart of every person, and that everyone struggles to liberate the God within himself?

It is also the deeper meaning of Christianity that the crucified one does not remain as he is, but rather he becomes the Awakening One!

In every human there are the seals of the cross—the hidden signs of the nails (the *chakras* of the yogis)—as centers of the Odic essence of the ego. In everyone an Odin-Christ awaits his Awakening. "Until Christ takes on a form in you," as is said in the Letter of the Galatians, the spiritual man struggles. He cannot rest contentedly under the coercion of material existence.

He is placed in matter to develop mastery over it, as Christ achieved his Mastery! It becomes not his grave but rather the gateway to a new birth. He transforms the matter of his body into the material of eternal rejuvenation, of the "Od." He does not destroy matter, but rather he imparts to it a vibratory form in himself that flows out into the Logos.

It remains the same material, it is just made accessible to its own foundation as a vibratory vortex of the solar spirit, of the constructive Lord in the material complex of the solar-system as it ultimately was proven and found to be by the scientific investigations of Thompson and Helmholtz.*)

And here the secret of the "Ninth Night" is now also revealed.

In a radiant solar vortex man appears beaming out of the light which is the soul of this system and its inwardly-turned eye! Liberated by a Rune of mysterious compelling power the solar wheel is unfolded into resounding, roaring life. The blood begins to sing in unfettered Runic energy. The word roars through all the fraternal spheres of the sun, all the souls connected, as if in a mighty organ tune shaking the vault of heaven.

The Ninth Night. . .

We devoutly stand before that which our forbears saw— the hanging man on the World-Cross descending for a new, joyous life, after his deadly tortures, into an eternal spring of ever-rejuvenating light.

---

*) In the so-called vortex-theory: "Matter is a dynamic vortex shape [G. *Wirbel*] in the aether, whose entire mass exists in continuous indestructible motion." (Dr. H. Fricke) "The planets represent this motion made visible in a way generally not visible in aetheric motion."

# II. The Ritual of the "Ninth Night"

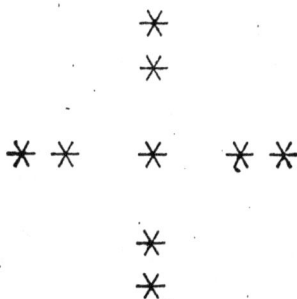

Figure 7

The messengers of this exalted being of light, the great antenna-cross in the "Swan"(14) (Fig. 7), the central radio-wave emitter in the cosmos, is represented by the sign of the Ninth Night. At one time the adepts of heaven sent a signal to it for humanity. It corresponds to a gigantic broadcast—or receiving antenna-structure (Fig. 7) in the sign of Cygnus, already recognized by the ancient wise-men of the *Vedas*, as well as by modern investigators, as the sign of the middle of the cosmos.

On it flash the waves of the spiritual lodge of the All. And whoever understands the language of these waves can speak daily and hourly with the spiritual brothers in the vicinity of this gigantic broadcast-cross. Is the Logos really still crucified on it, since we understand the speech that ignites meaning over vast spaces? Just as there are cable and and Morse-code signs in the earthly realm, the Runes are the Morse-signs in the cosmic world. They "rown" [whisper], i.e. they vibrate according to their position relative to this coordinating cross, just as Tiede (see above) indicated! The Runes are the secret sign-language of the spiritual lodge, of the "Hermes-Brothers"! But the human body is also an antenna-net and linking system full of communicative wires, full of articulate signs. Is telepathy anything other than becoming aware of them in conjunction with secret laws?

It is this that *Jesus rector* of the cosmic currents of intelligence taught his disciples: "Cast your nets out, that ye might catch the flashing *nunim*," which we, childishly enough, translate as "fish." *Nunim* are vibrating N-waves that echo*) in the body whenever these begin to speak in the cosmic language. They are the unfolding N-Rune-Secret relating to a cosmic set of laws and necessity: Nôt-Runa!

In the Egyptian *Book of the Dead* it says: "Behold, you dwell on the (radio)-stream of Kheraba,"— Kher-aba = "seat in the middle," "world-cross," "swan"— "there you shall gaze daily upon the reflected image of your face upon the waters," i.e. every day you carry your activity out into the Infinite, and cast out your net. . .

---

(*) Because a sound from above descends upon them.

Here, as there, we are talking about the inner expansion of an antenna-cross of an apparatus for the interplay of the ignition of the spirit over vast distances.

Truly a human being is the "most perfect physical apparatus" (Goethe). Everything we discover in nature is an outward projection of the inner man according to the law of psycho-physical parallelism. Everything, even the radiotelegraph, is within us. Therefore we create it in the outer world!

Nature is, according to Novalis, "a man unfolded"! But we do not owe this communicative wiring to the tender soul of some primeval she-ape, but rather to the invisible, learned voyagers in the ocean of light who installed it in us, i.e. to the Hermes-Brothers. They approached us upon hidden pathways and placed us in the Arga which saved us when the punishing, destructive waves destroyed the pithecoid men.

Whatever does not climb upwards will fall downward. Do not extend yourselves outward, but rather upward (Nietzsche). The *Edda* says that only the Valis and Vidars(15) will remain in the new world. These are the "elect" and "reborn," who are obedient to the spiritual radio-network that will transform their bodies into arks which will save them.

# III. The Night of Awakening

**First Operation**
The development of the first Runes as a broadcasting signal.

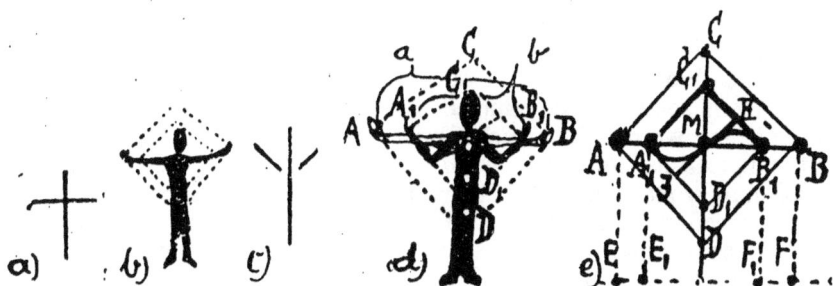

Figure 8

The signal-language of the Brothers of Hermes. The telepathic broadcasting and receiving "tabernacle."

Our egos form a radiotelegraphic system, a coordinated antenna-cross (Fig. 8a and b) of the type found in the great cross in Cygnus. (Fig. 7).

We are "crucified" in the language of the one Spiritual League in the All and we are subject to this League as prototypes. Their voice echoes in us according to very precise figures and awakens these figures in the vibrational field of our bodies.

We differentiate an outer and inner vibrational field, as we do in radiotelegraphy, in the sign of the Ninth Night (Fig. 7)— i.e. the cosmic antenna-cross of the communicative All-currents of the one spirit. According to this pattern the vibrational field (aura) of our bodies is also structures in layers.

First we enter into the outer vibratory field (Fig. 8b). We stretch our arms out in an antenna-like fashion and "tune in," to the receiver's basic tone: "A"— as line-waves are tuned in by an antenna. This tone corresponds to the cross among the so-called Chlandnic(16) tonal figures,*) i.e. the magnetic atoms of the Chlandnic tonal table arrange themselves in the shape of a cross. This is similar to what happens in the tonal field of our egos. The magnetic atoms of our outer vibrational field are arranged in the shape of a cross. "A" is the so-called "chamber-tone" of music. It vibrates at 432 cycles per second, i.e. the basic number of the so-called esoteric number system. As authors in practical esotericism have shown, the vibrations of the twelve primal concepts are to be derived from this. "A" is, however, also the tone of God in *Yah.*

---

*) These occur when one evenly spreads iron shavings over a glass plate and then strokes this plate with a violin bow thereby causing the glass to vibrate.

We awaken this sound in connection with the special words which, according to the *Edda*, awakened Wuotan as he brooded over the Need-Rune and then descended from the World-Cross (Fig. 7), thus the *Deus Mercurius,* or the Hermes Brotherhood, uses these to broadcast their first signals from the cosmic pole at the Cygnus-cross. These are just as precisely arranged as the linkages of radiotelegraphic vibratory systems, on the basis of so-called modular sounds.

In the *Edda* these words are:

*Æpandi nam* ("I took them up screaming," i.e. the Rune[s]).

These words are not just randomly selected but rather they carry with them something determined by cosmic laws! As it relates to the Logos, the words with which Christ died on the cross had the same meaning: *Ab-an'-dsaveh nesh'ma-y bi-yadika* ("Father, I commend my soul into your hands"). This is identical to how *Æpandi nam* is experienced in the Eddic ritual. The same spirit once more enters into his hands and he "takes it up," i.e. the Rune of Necessity (Old Norse *naudr* = Necessity).

There is actually a Law of the Logos contained here. If we make the sound *andi* (in *æp-andi*) in the right mental composure and sense of devotion, and develop it as a Logos, then the vibration of this syllable actually enters into our hands and reveals the secret of the *And*-Rune.

It is not the physiological vibration of a sound in the middle of the hands which we know from other Logos-exercises (see the author's *Wille und Konzentration*) that is decisive here, but rather the recognition of this vibration as an elementary effect of the Spirit of God as a genuine act of salvation.

Some sort of energy is breathed (Old Norse *anda* = breath) into the person here. Rightly understood this breath can not be rejected with the word "autosuggestion." The *Edda* makes this perfectly clear when it calls the "Warden of the *And*-energy (*And-Vari*) living in the material breath,*) the dwarf, or simply the material spirit. This dwarf explains everything that is spiritual as being suggestion, because it cannot comprehend the spiritual! Therefore And-vari guards access to the *And*- or Secret of the Spirit of God. Dwarven conceit first has to deny, and then misrepresent, any exalted phenomenon. Additionally, this And-vari is the materialistic mind in all of us, which denies everything spiritual.

He is resisting the exalted experience of the Ninth Night! The phenomenon that we will describe in the next chapter therefore will only make someone happy if he coerces the dwarf within himself, for such a one has the Need-magic, the Nôt-Ring (*Andvara-not* in the *Edda*) and holds it fast in his hand. The material spirit in us is not easily overcome, and yet it must be overcome! Even Siegfried, the German genius, was felled by the curse of the ring (see Wagner's *Ring des Nibelungen*), which he had wrested from the dwarf, after which he fell. But through the same magic, which kills and transforms, through the ancient holy Nôt-magic of the Ninth Night, he has to rise again!

This is the descent of Wuotan from the World-Tree, his liberation from the fetters of the cross (*drasil*).

---

*) Therefore infinitely small, "dwarf." Andvari is a "dwarf."

The mission of our folk begins with its national death, as did that of Christ. But above the cross that stands under the curse of the ring, of the black-elven Nibelung-power,*) of the dead Christ, there shines the Nazarene-Rune (Nôt-Rune): INRI. Until these four letters are endowed with energy and life, the murdered one will have to hang up there on the cross.

Nôt-magic both holds him fettered, and awakens him anew— this time, however, in a whole army of "Ein-heriars," those who, as we will show latter, take their name from En-hre, the oldest solar-city of the earth, On-Heliopolis, from the initiates of the ancient Aryan solar mysteries of the Egyptians.

In them the "recurrent breath" of the solar spirit (Tat, see *The Egyptian Book of the Dead* ch. I) plays a role, a spirit stimulated in the hands out of which this energy flows throughout the entire body of the Tattij (Hebrew *Dseddei* [pron. Jedd-eye],(17) Old German Tiudisco, Tuisto, the original name of the Germans [*Deutsche*].

With the magical sound *æp-andi* of the *Edda*, which can actually also mean "secret, spirit (*andi*) of the scream of need (*æp*)," to which Wuotan awakens and descends from the World-Tree, the same hidden "solar breath" returns.

Whoever finds its secret will rise up from the dead through it, but he first has to overcome the "material spirit," and the dwarf *And-vari* (Warden, Keeper of the *And*-Energy). Who can do this? If it has come to pass, however, then a certain energy will be breathed with every little word (*and*) into the seeker, into his hands actually— in which the recurring power lies ("Father I commend my spirit into thy hands"). And from the hands the entire body is saturated with the breath of rebirth. We explain this process by means of the antenna-like configuration of the arms (Fig. 8b), by means of which the body becomes a reception device for a telekinetic wave. So the "engagement" is material, but the function is a spiritual one. The cross-posture is the key to a higher spiritual community in many mystery schools. Why couldn't these communicate with one another by means of telekinetic currents just as we do today with technological means?

And there the little word *and* is a sort of key for the spiritual apparatus in man. It becomes a lever that, when pulled, causes the entire body to vibrate.

Experiment: We concentrate while sitting or walking on our feet, and at the same time speak the syllable *æp* at the end of each cycle of breath. We try to feel it in our feet. After a few exercises you will succeed. Your sense of touch is receptive for the working of the will; the antenna has been expanded down toward the fee. The word *pes*, "foot," is connected with the ability of the p-sound to effect a transference of power to the feet. The human body constitutes a letter-code apparatus. Whoever controls this apparatus can send out currents and radiotelegraphs with it into the invisible aether.

Once the vertical beam of the cosmic cross has been established there follows the second syllable *andi* to complete this part of the apparatus.

---

*) Nibelungs are dwarves here, not the noble gods.

Properly understood this principally concerns a mechanical act.

The material and spiritual belong together. "For this corruptible must put on incorruption" (I Corinthians 15:53). Faith became sterile in man because the laws of vibration were lost, because the material substratum was neglected by the believer. We repeat the exercise with the syllable *æp*. Now we further develop the syllable *andi* as follows: We speak the initial sound *an-* with a nasal resonance made through the nose. So, say *a-an*, while increasingly pressing your tongue against the upper palate and hold your spine in an increasingly more erect fashion. When it is fully raised to the level of the small of the back, we let the sound *an-n* end in a *-d*, i.e. make the shift *an-d*, transforming the resonance at the same time into a "d."

Now stretch your arms out horizontally (Fig. 8b) and try to feel the sound *and* in your hands as you repeat the exercise!

It will succeed— and you will start to feel this sound with a sucking sensation, an itching or prickling, warm or cool, in the middle of your hands. Concentrating at the same time we try to perceive the "i"-sound on the crown of our heads.

The antenna-cross has been spread out. We have become a receiver of the *and-* or spiritual-wave. But it remains questionable as to whether the ego, the owner of the apparatus, will be able to speak by means of it.

Here the "dwarf" comes into his own and guards against any unjust use of the apparatus, for such will become a burden for whomever uses this instrument in the wrong way.

We call this exercise that of the "outer vibratory circle" (a, Fig. 8d). The "inner vibratory circle" (b, Fig. 8d) cannot be opened by anyone. It is called the circle "pass-me-not." It cannot be opened, it only opens itself.

In it the absolute spirit rules, the singular spiritual essence of Christ.

The transition from one vibratory circle to the other is sealed by nine stars. (Fig. 8e) They contain the law of transformation in the "Ninth Night."

This transformation will be undergone by the whole of humanity, because, due to technology, mankind is now found under the jurisdiction of the outer ring. Like Prometheus, the founder of the "arts of fire," or technology, mankind has been fettered to a rock ACBD (Fig. 8d). Humanity has, like Prometheus, profaned the fire, for it is the "element of divinity"! Thus Need consumes mankind and gnaws at its loins until the miracle of a new form of salvation occurs.

Now we repeat the *Æp-andi* (or scream of Need) exercise and bring into contact the two respective circles in which the resonating and vibrating "nd"-sound (Need-Rune) was first made perceptible. This is the loin-cross which we make with the center of the hands in that we place these centers upon the lateral projections of the lumbar region at the hips. Here something strange will happen. A magnetic current begins to circulate in some people's bodies and to make itself felt as a sensation of magnetic attraction and tension in the hips. This perception will be heightened further if the eyes are lowered to the M-point in front of the chest. (Fig. 8d and e)

An electrical, telekinetic wave has been engaged. The physical projection apparatus has developed its initial activity. But the process should not be overestimated. It reamins uncertain as to whether the engaged wave is a "renegade" wave, whether rational or irrational. Here too the harmful currents are usually stronger than the good ones. Hysterics will easily manifest irritability in their entire systems, mediums will fall into "trances." Conversely a healthy person will manifest an increase in his entire energetic system along with the required vertical extension of the body in the sitting posture. With the right accumulation required for the completion of the experiment he will sense that something has occurred in his body, but the exact nature of this will only become known with progressive developments. Thus you will do well to undertake the Prometheus-grip at the loins, with caution, in order to perceive the pain of the devouring vulture.

When Jesus rose up again he commanded that his disciples place their hands on his hips in order for them to feel his renewed presence.

We do not know, however, whether this was done by them in *mysterium*, as we are showing it here, because Christ had really been resurrected but nevertheless it was also in *mysterium* in that he only appeared to those who were aware of him.

He also ascended in the flesh just like the one does to whom the sign of the feeling in the hips manifests, and who thus enters into a condition of a carnal transformation and rebirth.

With this the first operation of the Ninth Night is complete— the Odization of the person by means of telekinetic, magnetic currents. The Æp-andi, or Nôt-Rune, has developed its first form of energy. The currents respond. The cross is laid out. The Hermes-Brothers communicate. They rotate the solar wheel and it breathes its breath out over toward the expectant ones— into their hands, their chests, and their hips.

It is the Nôt-Rune which has set this into motion, however, for only those who attract the currents with desire, suffering, longing and hunger will be impregnated by them! And only to those will these currents come. Therefore those who suffer Need are richer than anyone else, for their Need has won a voice and an "An"-swer [G. *Ant-wort*] from the realm of the redeemer. . .

# IV. Essence of the Receptive Wave
# The Asur-Esoterium

The Telekinetic Energy of the Second Rune.
The second verse of the rune-song relates to this:
"A second I learned,    that people need,
who wish to become physicians."
(Hávamâl,
Wodan's Rune-Knowledge)
Housed in this Rune is the ancient sign of salvation used by the Sons of Mercury (Hermes-Brothers), the so-called staff of Mercury, caduceus:

cf. Figure 8c, which, as the so-called sign of Aesculapius, still serves as the symbol of the healing and medical professions today. In the mysteries (cf. the author's work *Konzentration und Wille*, ch. 3, Fig 2) it originally related to the captured waves of Mercury or Hermes-Thoth, which those with knowledge know how to use. In any event they had their own law that did not obey the human intellect, but rather it was a law which humans had to accommodate. The wave redeems, but it also destroys with severe delusion and selfishness anyone who tries to bend it to his will with any recurring effort. Only pure self-dissolution in thought, devoted love in knowledge, a bowing to the spirit of *truth*, leads to its recognition. Only to such a person will it wed itself and become a mighty tool in the hands of a future humanity. For it is the lightning bolt (cf. Fig. 8e) of the God-man, which unerringly strikes that which is of a lower nature and obliterates it. It is the mental or spiritual wave itself in its pure form of the time-space progression. In the *Asur-* or *Ansur*-secret, which is also known as Arahi-Sof-UR (ASUR), it takes the second position, that of the S-Rune. *Ansur* or *Asur* is an old name of Wuotan, which already appears among the Babylonians as "Ansur" (Mercurius-Nebo), who corresponds to Kisar (Kissosos) or the Earthly Star (Lord), Saturn (Ki-un).

Ethically Ansur is the same as *Na-sir*, that is the name of a highly evolved entity which returns only in order to alleviate and dissolve*) Need. In the form of a so-called bind-rune it consists of the great tetrad of the Runes:

---

*) *Nirmana-kaya* among the Indians.

This represents the tabernacle or tent of the higher man (*Armanen, Saemanen*), the so-called "Armanic hut," by means of which Wuotan-Mercurius descends in the Ninth Night. We see this hut represented in Figure 8e, in which we also find the vibratory forms of these Runes. They are living forces in the tele-organism of man. "To be in their hut" means to participate in the eternal spiritual forces of creation, it means to complete the cross and descend as a living being.

In the

## second operation

of the Ninth Night this hut opens, as the holy texts of the Egyptians say, "the tomb of the god, in order to allow the light to stream in."

The protective coat, Svalin, is the solar shield. The uplifting wave of sal-vation (*sal* and *sig* named as a Rune):

is something spiritual, not material. It only exists in the conceptual world, but exists also in the conceptual world of the universal Hermes-Brotherhood (Mercury-Venusians) of our entire solar-system which is saturated with spiritual streams. This Rune is encoded in our bodies with a sign, which, if properly presented, is unfolded at once and the solar-wheel:

begins to revolve.*)

We repeat the first and second operations, as indicated, and bring the words:

*æp-andi nam*

into vibration on the antenna-cross (Fig. 8a and b).

We await the *an*-swer. But this will not follow from merely tuning in. This has only installed the instrument. The second word, *nam*: "he took up" contains the so-called Barrow [G. *Berg*]-Rune. It still conceals [G. *verbirgt*] something: "he took them up screaming of Need. . . *æpandi nam.*" But in this "taking" or "gathering up" [G. *Auflesen*]**) of the runes lies the beginning of the awakening of the divine self.

First the one and then the other, as the second operation is completed after the first, something is taken up in the hips— a pain, the felling of fetters, of being bound: "screaming in need he took them up."

But the same hand that takes away the felling of pain in the hips here is now transformed by the force of the second Rune (of the An-s-ur of the S-Rune) into that of a shield and protection. The ascension begins as does a turning of the tide.

---

*) For this is known by the two S-Runes contained in it "*Sal* (salvation) and *Sieg* [G. victory]."
**) The German word *lesen* [reading] is derived from *auflesen* [gathering up] of the runes.

The feeling of restriction and tension in the hips due to the influx of the *Sint*-waves will disappear as soon as the Will seizes these currents. The purpose of all the Need and suffering was actually to stimulate the Will and stretch it to a higher level.

This higher Will is given over to the longing and desire to become one with the eternal world of the spirit. By means of this higher Will and desire we are now actually able to overcome the Od-flame (wound of Prometheus) that had burned in our hips and which had bound us in suffering to the power of the Need-Rune. The perceived Od-glow is a material substance subordinate to the imagination. We have actually just generated it by means of the imagination by closing the chain and making ourselves into an oracular telescope ASBD (Fig. 9a). The current quivered in us and began to rock us like a table. But all of this remains merely an enduring of the *Sint*-wave.

Now, while grasping the hips, we generate an imaginative construct, the Eddic solar-shield (Sva-lin), out of this out-flowing Od-flame (out of the suffering as Od-in is being born). We generate it by means of conceptualization as a great shield in the form of a hollowed-out hand, only bigger than the natural shape, situated in front of the torso. The generation of this shield as a protective coat against the ruinous effects of the flame is absolutely necessary for

> "Mountains and fields would burn
> if it ever fell from his hand."

*Edda* [Grímnismál 39]

It is called, in a somewhat concealed manner, the "solar-shield," but this indicates the inner sun, the "solar-plexus," the energies of which begin to be exteriorized during the performance of this first hand-grip. These energies "emerge." The ego can generate forms from this spiritual material, something like those yogis known as *hamsas* do, who exteriorize Od and evoke different entities out of it; or like a hypnotist, who is unconsciously working with an exteriorized neural substance through which he entrances his medium.

Here the important thing is to become the master of the flame. It can rage unfettered with the power of inordinate desire, but subdued by a civilized Will it becomes a high — or even the highest — power in the hands of humanity.

We all will, to speak in terms of Faust, at some point approach the gate "out of whose mouth flames all of Hell," for Faust is the *Zeit-Geist* [spirit of the age], the way of every ego in the present-day.

The only one who will be able to come out of the present-day deluge [*Sint-Flut*] is the one who recognizes the waves being sent and who forms them into a protective "*Ar-k*." This is what we are reading about here.

All of us become ill due to the out-flowing flame of degenerating, agitated nervous energy, i.e. *Mut-spilli* ("split-mood")(18) and life force.

In the *Edda* the old world goes down in the flames of Muspell. Originally "Muspell" is the greatest creative word of the Logos, but in our present-day this very word is being ruined.

All of us must enter into the Ninth Night with Odin in order to alleviate this condition of suffering. Then the transformation will take place. The ruinous flames of Muspell will be fettered, through knowledge the Send-Wave will be made into an energy in the service of the Will.

This is how we form the hollowed-out solar-shield in front of our chests: After the second operation we imagine ourselves sitting upright within a concave shield in the form of a large hand which covers the whole of the front part of our bodies down to the pelvic region. In this way the solar-plexus in the pit of the stomach is to be in the conceptual middle of the concave right hand reaching down from above. Breathing deeply we seek to accommodate ourselves to the hand conceived of in this way. We breathe ourselves evenly into a feeling of tranquility in which the self-created shield arises.

With it begins the growth, the development of a new essence in the person, a new embryonic process. The ego attaches itself to this shield like a placenta and is nourished by the shining streams of milk coming from an invisible divine mother.

It is proper to stick with the placenta until the new birth is completed and always keep your focus on this protective shield. For now the "Nine Mothers," or nourishing original streams of light, will forthwith reveal themselves to us. These are represented by the nine mother-staves of the High-song:

Figure 9c

The runic nomenclature as symbolic key of the language of Mercury.
The magical tetractys.

Now we will see how these signs interplay and bring about the connection with the Hermes-Brothers.

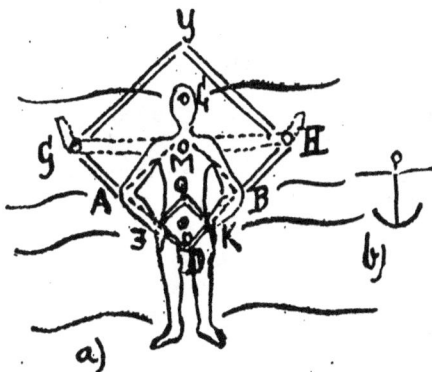

Figure 9

The radiotelegraphic arrangement within the human being.
The Secret of "Ygg-drasil"
b) The antenna-anchor

# V. The Ritual of the "Ninth Night"
## Second Operation

The ego, transformed into a net for tele-conductive currents of "*And-*" or spiritual waves, is what we have experienced up to this point. And this rare "current-net" (see Fig. 9b) was already called the Tree of Life (see Fig 6) among the ancient Persians and Chaldeans. Man lives eternally on it, for it is in "tele-conduction" with the highest creative forces — the *And-* or spirit-waves — in all the cosmos. They are generated by thinking people, but they have been there in nature from the beginning— for the first spiritual beings that thought anything initially generated these waves and then became an antenna-like body for the next generation. Thus the wave "propagated" itself. And thus even today the spirit-being called man "propagates" himself by means of the spiritual wave of generative energy!

This is the law of our "divinization." But if our reception ceases in the circulation of the spiritual wave of generative energies, then we will fall off of the tree — withered and worthless — and nature will make us into mere "matter" and into manure for her continuing forms of life.

There are people who are nothing more than "manure" in nature— but not *seed*. *Seed* is the spiritually generative and tele-kinetically functioning substance that we recognize in Figure 9 as the CMD configuration. It represents the central conductor of all tele-conductive currents in and around us— the *sympathikus*! When we stretched out the antenna in GH (Fig. 9a), we already unfolded its higher power, the ability to attract things from All-spirit, something which Scheiermacher called "love." A modern seeress, Selma Jäger (*Die neue Rasse*, self-published, Ihlfeld in the Harz) characterizes the *sympathikus* as a "neural sun." In fact there are people in whom this mysterious sun "shines" or gives off energies, and these people continuously release currents of blessing and healing by means of such a conductor within them for their fellow men. In them there lives a higher nature from which they themselves are generated — conducted and functioning across space — which has been installed into their solar-plexus in which God himself has been condensed— the all-generative spiritual being.

There is only one spirit, just as their is only one kind of each force in nature. There aren't two "electricities," nor two kinds of "warmth," so there is only one spirit! And an All-current-spirit-net "vibrates throughout" nature, i.e. Ygg-drasil: *yggr* = vibrate, tremble and *drasil* = "cross" or "carrier" of these vibrations. We too are stretched out on this All-current-spirit-net and the gods— eternally living, living consciously and reawakening are in it.

The ritual depicted above is treated by, among others, the Egyptians in their holy writings and it was the founding ritual of the Hermes-Brotherhood. "The sun rises in the grave of the god," it is said there— the neural sun is ignited in the material body and begins to shine, to "rayify." Thus Odin also goes to Mimir, and he finds the spiritual eye M (Fig. 9) in his body. Another eye, a god's eye, resides in his forehead— the third eye (pineal gland, *sahasvara*). However, Mimir is the guardian of a secret that is older than the gods. He belongs to ta pre-divine family of nature-spirits. Odin has to go to him. In speech he has to exchange runes of wisdom with him— runes of necessity that will remain even if the gods pass away.

Thus he will find the first of all the Runes at the Well of Wisdom belonging to Mimir. We too approached this well. What we accomplished was the act of looking within into an all-seeing eye in ourselves, into a hidden solar-eye. There was a verbal exchange with this eye, just like that of Wuotan and Mimir, a murmuring of ancient secrets: *Æpandi nam*. . .

The sun will enter the sign of Aquarius for the next two thousand years. This Aquarius ("water-bearer") is, according to Finn Magnusen, the "Mimir" of the Germanic peoples, Odin is the solar-spirit. Thus again mankind re-discovers the pre-divine eye which has been submerged into his material body. Therewith a profound transformation is completed. The divine essence, which has died away in cultic practices has been transformed into something which is greater by nature and something primeval [*Ur-Erstes*]. This divine essence strips its outer garment away and becomes something primevally eternal [*Ur-Ewig*] in nature.

*Ygg-drasil* is the eternal spiritual growth in the All, the functioning of the spirit as one of the highest forces of nature from the beginning of things. As we discovered during the first ritual procedure in the initial operation of the Ninth Night, we are already, from the beginning, an ego which began to reflect objects— just as the first spiritual *manas* in the interior of any given body (Fig. 8 and 9) began to vibrate and as an initial spiritual pole of perception in nature was established. But then we began as the first Rune of wisdom says: *Æpandi nam*, "to take up," the Runes, the seal of eternity in all things; from the magnetic pole inside man currents flow outward to all beings, with hidden threads to connect man to everything that exists. Everything shines up through the magical power of that Rune and is drenched with an eternal glow— with a hidden divine force in nature.

We came to understand ourselves in the *And*-energy (by means of the Need-Rune or Rune of Necessity) as we actually incarnate it, allowing it to stream through our spines by the power of a spiritual conduction of breath. That was the experience of the first operation! Out of suggestive phenomena there progressively develops something real. The Need-Rune, perceived by us as a vibration,*) becomes flesh (matter), is assimilated to our whole being and thereupon we depart the first circle of existence to which that which was necessary had banished us and in which we struggle against this Necessity, as we perceive it to be a Need, pain and resistance.

The dwarf allows us into the second circle. We overcome the world of Need, which is only possible because the great spiritual primeval vibration that floods through all existence, and upon all those who are attuned to it at the highest tone, was stilled and subdued in us. Attracted now by this tone, stretched on it like the highest string of the world-harp, gripped by it right down to our hearts, the transformation occurs.

---

*) *And*-vibration, as we showed.

But only real Need, real suffering and desire, can be transformed into a new and eternal bliss (Sanskrit *ananda*). This Need is recognized in the first operation of the Ninth Night as one still feels bound by the runic compulsion. You feel, in an occult sense, your "crucifixion in matter." But the lightning bolts of a new, more satisfactory, world-order are already flashing to you. The invisible tongues of fire are already working on you— the waves of a still unintelligible language. Then you take the Rune up, as it says in the "High Song" of the *Edda*: *Æpandi nam*. This *nam* ("he took") indicates an esoteric process.

You take them up, bowing down and saying *æp-andi*. Therein lies the *esoterium*, the movement of the spine while intoning the *andi*-sound, the "invertebration" (cf. the work *M-Wellen* by the author).

In the skaldic art the Runes are cast before the soothsaying priest who "takes them up," inspired by the magnetic currents that flash within him. This is how we experienced it in the first phase of the operation on Ygg-drasil, the world-cross (Fig. 8b), so it is also repeated here. By means of certain devotional exercises and rituals the ego is made receptive for a particular kind of spiritual impulse— in this case that of the Hermes-Brotherhood.

Thus the second operation now shows us the secret of proper selection and reception. There are nine main Runes as powers of the nine spheres ("Mothers") together with their negative correspondences they make eighteen.

In these eighteen Runes the law of necessity functions, but in each Rune there is the knowledge of its rulership over this secret.

What began with the N- or Need-Rune is concluded with the highest one, the Rîta-Rune.(19) It demonstrates the completion of the law. Rîta is a symbol of the attainable divine freedom into which the Aryan is placed, but which usually cannot be attained because the Nôt-magic in the hand of the demon, the Ring "Andvara-nôt" prevents it. But here we show the way to overcome this "Guardian of the *And*-Force" in that we voluntarily submit ourselves, submerge it in our own egos and thus make it possible to attain a new over-coming by means of our own Will.

And this is now the

**second operation**

of the Ninth Night: The grasping of the ring and bursting it asunder!

# VI. The Tele-Language of the Hermes-Brotherhood (Wuotan) and their Morse-Signals

We have already learned how to produce the first three of the following signals and have become receptive to the corresponding forces of the universal Brotherhood of Hermes.

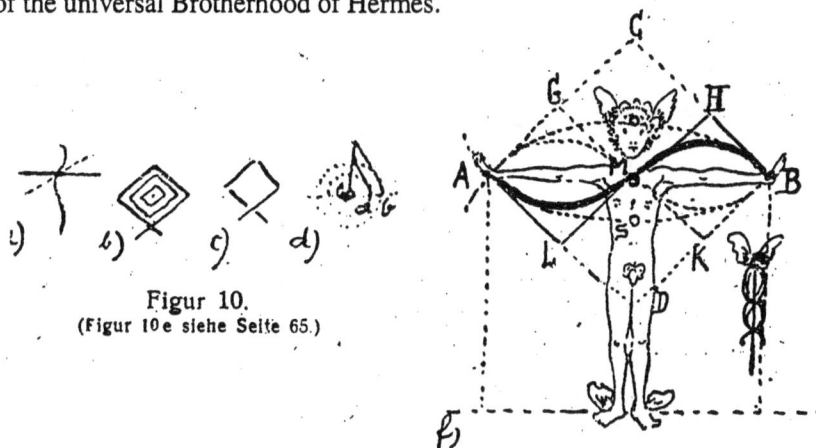

Figur 10.
(Figur 10e siehe Seite 65.)

Figure 10

Thus all Runes represent certain tele-conductive symbols in the vibratory sphere of the body. Whoever "embodies them in the way they are supposed to be embodied according to the teachings of Armanism (Irmin, Arman is the Hermes of the Germans), will come into contact with the corresponding powers of the Brothers of the Hermes-League. The great, invisible spiritual community, the "Kingdom of Heaven," prepares the way.

In Figure 10 a) represents the installation of the antenna-cross, in which the vertical is here represented with a curved line standing for the spine; for the spine which represents the vertical beam of the cross is not a straight line, but rather a curved one. In ancient esoteric tradition it is usually signified by a snake. In the bible as well the descending serpent that seduces Eve is a *"Sint-wave"* and is also shown to be such on an ancient Babylonian seal (see Menant *Recherches glyptiques*).

The *Sint*-wave is bound*) to the body — "invertebrated"— and we recognize the syllables *and-, ans-***) (Nôt-Runa) as the invertebration-motif. Among the yogis the speaking and breathing of the word *hansa* (*ha-ansa*) represents the process of invertebration. Among the ancients Chonsu-Dioysius serves the same function, and the "Dionysian" in the writings of Nietzsche is an attempt to come into contact with the language of the Hermes-Brothers (which bear the three secret sigils: "Zeret-ust-ari," i.e. "Zarathustra," the great spiritual triangle of the zodiac in the list of decans, see *Yoga-Praxis* by the author).

---

*) It is similar to a snare that is lowered over the person from above. This is how Jesus describes the new day of mankind as well. (Luke 21:35)
**) Hebrew Enos, Jesus calls himself the "Son of Enos."

The Frenchman Victorien Sardou portrayed, while in a "Dionysian state" (practicing trance-painting), the House of Zarathustra on the planet Jupiter (see Flammarian, *Unbekannte Naturkräfte*). There is one on a moon of Jupiter as well, and perhaps this "house" also exists on Venus and Mercury, for as we learn from the decan-lists, Zeret-ust-ari signifies an astral figure, a so-called trigon, in which certain influences work and are transmitted to the earth according to ancient astrological rules. In the decan-lists (the most ancient figure of the sky) the so-called earthly trigon is signified by Capricorn-Virgo-Taurus, but by means of the procession of the equinoxes this now corresponds to the "spiritual triangle": Aquarius-Libra-Geminii.

There are three fixed mathematical places in the energy belt of the solar system, in the so-called zodiac, in which the interplanetary influences (i.e. the influences flowing among the planets) are transmitted. It is the house in which all other houses rest, represented by a triangle or tower Δ, and this is why even Nietzsche sees a man coming from a tower (in the so-called tightrope dancer scene) at the beginning of his *Also sprach Zarathustra*.

The vision is to be traced back to the appearance of the Hermes-Brotherhood with the aid of an astral shift, i.e. the entrance of the sun into the sign of Aquarius, and thus into the spiritual trigon.

Also the most glorious sayings that Nietzsche provides here about the "Cry of Need" of the higher man, about the liberating will: "When ye desire with a single will, and your Need also becomes a Necessity for you," etc., point to Hermes-mysteries. In opposition to the softening venal Venusian influences (the Vanic gods of the *Edda*) here the more austere, more serious and more thoughtful ones of Mercury (the "Aryan" ones under the leadership of Wuotan in the *Edda*) successfully make their way.

A shattering "will to power" is to be recommended as an arouser and inciter of humanity. The emotional element of the Vanes (Venusians) has exercised a softening and spoiling influence on faith (as an emotional excitation, not as an inspirational energy, which it was originally). This influence should be avoided because humanity is not yet mature enough for the high sensuality of the Venusians, or "Uranides."

The will to power is actually not a final goal, but a transitional stage, and the present-day struggle for power is its realization. But behind all this stands the "I-serve" idea of the White Brotherhood.

Now in the second sign (Fig. 10b and c) the so-called older O- or Oe-Rune (Odr, Od, Odin) of the rune-alphabet is depicted. It is the receptive plane (Fig. 9) that is formed in the first operation of the Ninth Night in which Odin-Influence decidedly came into play— the "Odization" (= magnetizing) of the ego by tele-kinetic currents (Send-waves) with the aid of a certain configuration. This is generated from within by the one doing the exercise.

In the film already mentioned above, *Herrin der Welt* ("Ophir"), which shows some real inspiration, the heroin of the drama is drawn by means of certain signs to "Ophir" and his great treasure of gold hidden in the earth. In the film this magical force is depicted by a sigil similar to that found in Fig. 10b. This sign is acquired by an old rabbi in East Asia with great effort on his part and despite risks to his life.

The gold hoard portrayed here is similar to that of the "Nibelungen" in the German saga. That treasure was sunk near Worms (the worm [= serpent] city on the Rhine, cf. the "worm" in Figure 10a which brings it back) and which will also be rediscovered in its own time. But more precisely it corresponds to the hoard of the Amelungs into whose hands this treasure was delivered when the sun entered the sign of Aquarius (in terms of the decans "Im-la," from which Amelung is derived, Germanic "gim-le" = "upper heaven"), the Nibelungs*) abducted their power and handed it over to the Amelungs.

In that film "Ophir" is the Rose-City of the "Queen of Saba," who is called Sh'wa in the original text of the Bible (II Chronicles 9:1), and indicates an original location of the Sabean solar-cult (see Sh'waaeg = "solar breath," "solar spirit" above). (On the star-cult of the Sabeans see Chwolsohn, *Sabäer*.) Here the heroin of the drama is crowned as Astarte, which likewise indicates the Sun-Goddess, more precisely the eternally rejuvenating light Ostara, Ishtar (see *Yoga-Praxis* by the author). But for the coming of Hermes-Christianity this word means much more. It is the key to all the higher solar mysteries and is so by virtue of the primeval healing Rune that underlies it: *Uste, oste* or in Sanskrit *su-astika* (swastika), Fa-uste = *faustum* (*quod felix faustumque sit*), in the name "Faust," additionally in the manifestation of the disease caused by an *uste*-force— "hysteria"!

The *Uste*-Rune (in "Ostara") represented in Figure 10d indicates the energy on the solar-wheel (swa-ustika), an energy which causes the wheel to turn and **thanks to the Uste-energy** awakens it to life.

The *Os*-or *Oste*-Rune first of all indicates the Ases, i.e. the *vis intelligibilis solaris*. Empedocles called this same energy in the solar system the tangential energy as a propelling energy working from the circumference of a circle, from the outside inward, in the direction of a tangent. According to Figure 10d it is contained in the two levers of the *Uste*-Rune — a and b. The inner vibratory ring b (Fig. 8d) transfers to the outer vibratory ring (a) by means of its constant action. If this process is envisioned as a living one in which there is a constantly active energy working from the outside inward, then the impression will be gained of the profound meaning of the *Os*- or *Oste*-Rune in Armanism. In the past an attempt was made with the aid of these Runes to investigate those things which we today try to discover in mathematics or physics, and it would be a great mistake to try to deny that our ancestors had knowledge of the most important laws and forces of nature. To the contrary, they had a deep and spiritual comprehension of these things even if this knowledge was not so intellectual.

Certainly their language and comprehension is usually symbolic in its outer form. Despite this they knew what, for example, the differentiation of a line or curve was. As the circular movement of the inner circle K (Fig. 10d) transfers to the outer one in the way we have discussed, the circle proceeds in its vibration toward the outside, and thus passes through each individual point along the line ab, as is shown in Figure

*) Taurean families of Venus. Their rulership began with the entrance of the spring equinox in the sign of Taurus about 6000 years ago. The high-point of their regime was in Aries, Nef (Knef), Egypto-Atlantean "ram-god." (See Wilkinson *Manners of Egypt*).

10d. Thereby there occurs a differentiation of this line as a result of circular movement, i.e. the line is touched and differentiated in all its individual points by the progressing circular movement, It is "vibrated" by them throughout. This is especially insightful when we think of this analytical process as being transferred to a physical system, such as that of leverage-energies as understood in engineering. In their symbolic language our ancestors designed infinitely small breaks in the line CB (Fig. 10d), along which the circular movement rhythmically proceeds and ascends as "thorns."

The Ase is therefore in possession of a "thorn," with which he exercises a magical power.

The magical thorn, which also transmitted knowledge of divine knowledge on Sinai, is in ancient mysticism therefore nothing other than the principle of differentiation— only it's not purely intellectual here, but rather — a layer deeper — conceived of with emotion and will as an *engagement* into the *divine will!*

Leibnitz, who discovered differentiation (segmentation of a line into absolute "units" or "monads"), already saw in this law the key to all theodicy (justification of the divine cosmic order through knowledge of nature). He wanted to present the mathematical "function," which was built upon differentiation, as the basis and essence of the law of causality, something which Wundt continued in modern cognitive theory. In fact this postulate is the key to the ancient mysteries for those who do not see in it merely a mystification of religious thought.

The "law of causality" or "law of necessity," which can torture the ignorant and destroy humanity, ultimately depends on an intellectual act, on a recognition, in order that it can lead to salvation!

This recognition is signified in the *Edda* by the appearance of the "thorn" at the darkest time of humanity (*Hrafna-galdr*). Whoever recognizes it then will be saved, like those who recognize the serpent of salvation on the cross (Numbers 21:9, Fig. 10a) and Christ, who is characterized as the serpent of salvation in the New Testament (John 3:14).

We met with this "lifting up of the serpent on the cross" (see Fig. 10a) when we ourselves became serpents— along our spines, which has a serpentine line and curve as we erected the antenna-cross.

The serpent was put up on the cross. Now the question arises: Does the Hermes-Brotherhood hear us, do they send us a "sign" that they hear us?

According to esoteric tradition the "an"-swer lies in a very particular "sign," knowledge in a particular experience. Here that which has been longed for occurs! Phenomena experienced through auto-suggestion do not make this happen, but rather it is a concurrence by means of a spiritual act which becomes, by the very nature of the experience, a completely unambiguous event for the one who experiences it.

The wave is "anchored" in the person. We see this "anchor" in Figure 9b and the "configuration" that corresponds to it in Figure 9a. We showed the **second operation** which is to be undertaken so that the "anchoring" of the ego occurs in the *send*-wave. He who really suffers and bears Need, and in whom an inner hand will reach up from below with desire, will also experience connection and unification here. The Need-Rune can only save those who are in Need, not those who are already satisfied. That which the latter experiences remains auto-suggestion, but what the former experiences is truth. The feeling of *truth* is admixed with their knowledge. A trembling from within, a shock to the ego (in the sense of the *Uste*-Rune), a unique vibration is perceptible while, as we have indicated, the hand-centers — attuned to the tone of the *And-* or Need-Rune — are unified with the hip-centers (see Fig. 9a). A circulation is generated on the inside. The *Sint*-wave takes on a specific vibratory configuration, ADBM (Fig. 9a and b), in which it takes up the body— that of the saving "ark."

The body has become a radiotelegraphic receiver for a higher type of wave.

We have learned to communicate *telepathically* with a still invisible community of spirits. Now we will try to look more deeply into their "Morse-code."

To begin with this involves directing the captured waves by means of an act of will. For it is here the value of these waves is ascertained. If it is of a lower kind it will seek to constrain us. If it is of a higher kind we will constrain it and control it with our wills. That which seeks to enslave us cannot be of a higher kind, because the divine works upon us in such a way that makes our wills free. Thus we experience what Nietzsche proclaims: "O, thou my will, turn every need, thou my necessity."

The third transformation of the Need-Rune, Need into "Thorn," shown in the previous chapter then leads to the liberation of our wills, to the awakening to the Thorn-Rune.

We repeat the **second operation** of the Ninth Night.

If the auto-imaginative current of the golden rectangle ADBM has been generated and if we have mastered it, then we seek to transform it into a flowing, living energy by means of our will. At first we will perceive it only as tension. If it is not present merely as suggestion, but on the contrary we feel that it has been generated by auto-imagination and that a real vibration has begun to be felt in the interior of the body or in the hip-region, then we will attempt to generate the so-called "golden chain of truth." In esoteric tradition this is also called the "golden chain of H'omer" (H'omer is "Logos, Word, Truth" in the Kabbalah).

The first square, which we evoked by means of the positioning of our arms as we touched our hips, was ADBM. The second square, which at the same time forms the fourth part of the first square and which lies between the hip-points, was IDKM, the third between the outstretched arms GH, is GYHD.

All three golden rectangles are connected to one another through a vibration, through a magical runic energy, and contain within themselves the treasures of all the waves, the Gold of Ophir. Therefore they are also unified in the Seal of Ophir, see Figure 10b.

The second Rune, developed out of the *And*-Rune, is the *Fa-, Hva-Hwa*-Rune, and is contained in the name of the guardian dwarf: And-vari. It embodies the life-force through which the vibration of a center is brought forth, and a circular motion toward the exterior results, see Figure 10d. Empedocles called this primeval universal force the tangential-force, and in fact we can also demonstrate it through the effect of one or several tangents upon the mid-point of a circle, C (see 10d).

As a result of this emerging movement in the life-center (C) the tangent makes a transition from position (a) to position (b). The center begins to vibrate, which symbolically announces the Life-Rune *Fa* (pronounced "hva" or "hwa"). But it also becomes the Rune of the *conservation*, of protection (Old Norse *vari*), and self-preservation with regard to all spiritual life-values— the *truth*!

It is for this reason that we said above that after the capture of the current, the truth shall be separated from the lie, knowledge of what is essential from that which is mere appearance.

This occurs in connection with the following summary process: The second operation, shown in Figure 9a, is to be repeated. The captured *Sint*-wave begins to circulate in the body and the antenna-apparatus begins to work. As your hands make contact with the hip-points in I and K (Fig. 9 and 10), you construct a small circle IDKM (Fig. 9) between the hip-points. This small circle is conceived of as constantly increasing in size as a result of the influx of energy from the Fa-Rune, as indicated. Now the key lies in this *Hva*-Rune itself. If you pronounce the syllable "hva" slowly and observe yourself as you do so, you will notice that your mouth passes through increasingly wide degrees of openness as you pronounce the syllable.

Now the key word of the Hermes-Brotherhood develops, by means of this word they become known to humanity and give us the an-swer [*Ant-wort*]: Band of Truth [*Bund des Wahren*]. You actually speak the word "band," just as you did with "*and*" in And-vari or Æp-andi, allowing the word to flow up your back in you imagination, as we discussed above, until it reaches your lumbar region. At the same time you stretch your hands out in a cross-formation and perceive the echo of the syllable "band" in the middle of your hands. You close the circuit, as shown, and sit perfectly erect firmly on your hips, as you will feel a tension or magnetic gravitation in your body. At the same time you should gaze upon the middle point (M) of the rectangle ADBM created by this position as if it were a magical pane of glass— remain sitting absolutely and perfectly erect as the pronunciation of the "band"-motiv dictates, for only in this way is the bond with the Hermes-Brotherhood produced. As you grasp your hips the middle of your hands must rest on the hip-bones, but your fingers should point downward to the ground, that is, vertically and along the "trouser seam" in a manner similar to that of the old Prussian military stance. The position must be an absolutely straight one and the chin is to be pulled in to the chest.

Now you release your hands from the hip-surface and bring them into the position G and H, Figure 9— that is, horizontal, as in the first cross-posture. But stretch them out toward the front in such a manner that they are parallel in their longitudinal axes (mid-hand axes), Figure 9, with the longitudinal axes of the feet.

Then speak the second syllable *of* [German *des*] concentrating in this same posture and attempting to feel it in your hands and feet at the same time. After a few times of trying this you will get a feeling of soaring upward. At that point speak the phrase "of the Truth" [*des Wahren*], as you allow your mouth to go through ever increasing degrees of openness it is only then that you gaze upon the central point, and then, when the circles of increase corresponding to the rectangles that are becoming ever larger rise ever upward with the midpoints on the spine from D to C, you let the sound "hwas" strive as it flows back from the cross (i.e. reversed from the sound "band") to take its place again in the center within the chest and from there it moves laterally into the hands G and H. During all this your body always remains erect. Also do the same thing with the sound "swah-r" (a contraction of *es wahr* [it (is) true]).

The force works in a pulling fashion toward the outside, tangentially, as a result of ovulation (increasing circulation) but it also draws inward and tries to unite both tendencies.

This is the *esoterium* of the ancient An-s-ur-Rune which points to the Ase, as returning through the magical force of these Runes to the "Na-sir" in INRI (see above) and liberation from the cross. For it is at this point the Hermes-Brothers answer. In our language, however, this process is indicated by the formula: "In the bond of truth" [*Im Band des Wahren*].

In all of this it is to be sure necessary that you do not think of yourself as merely speaking "words" here, but rather you are speaking in *spirit*, for it is in the spirit that the decisive function lies!

The suggestive sense-dream — one into which the ego gleams, removed from the World-Tree of a great brotherhood unified by love — is dissolved by a feeling of tranquility in an exalted power extending throughout the universe. This spiritual breath into which you step is the truth. All spirits have been bound together in it throughout all eternity. Truth and love are two aspects of the same thing, the first belongs to the spirit, the second to the emotions. Truth effects the attraction (love) of entities in the spirit, and thus we have entered into such a community. Now in all this, truth, as understood in purely psychological terms, is the unification of all tangentials and centripetal vibrations of souls. We experienced this in the previous experiment. And there ensues something that cannot be described, but rather can only be experienced. The indicated dilemma of two spiritual powers, of centrifugal *desire* and centripetal *knowledge* and *thought* is resolved. Desire and knowledge melt into one, the ego traverses the restrictive circle and enters into the universal brotherhood, the true *Bol-sh'wa*-Congregation(20) which conducts the mystery of the solar-breath (*shwa*) under its banner.

Thus one speaks these words during every operation with the attention to the attunment of body and soul and the vibration of the Logos:

"In the Band of Truth my hearted is opened.
I feel, welling up and flowing through my body,
The spring of the one inexorable life.
I stand in the power of the Eternal One"
                    *Ansur - Arahi - sof -ur*
"In the Band of Truth my ears are opened.
I hear each and every entity speak,
Even those dwelling in my own body
And vibrating they circulate with soft tones."
                    *Ansur - Arahi - sof -ur*
"In the Band of Truth my mouth is opened,
I speak the words of eternal being myself
And feel in myself an eternally persistent weaving
Of the One Power, which lovingly permeates me."
                    *Ansur - Arahi - sof -ur*

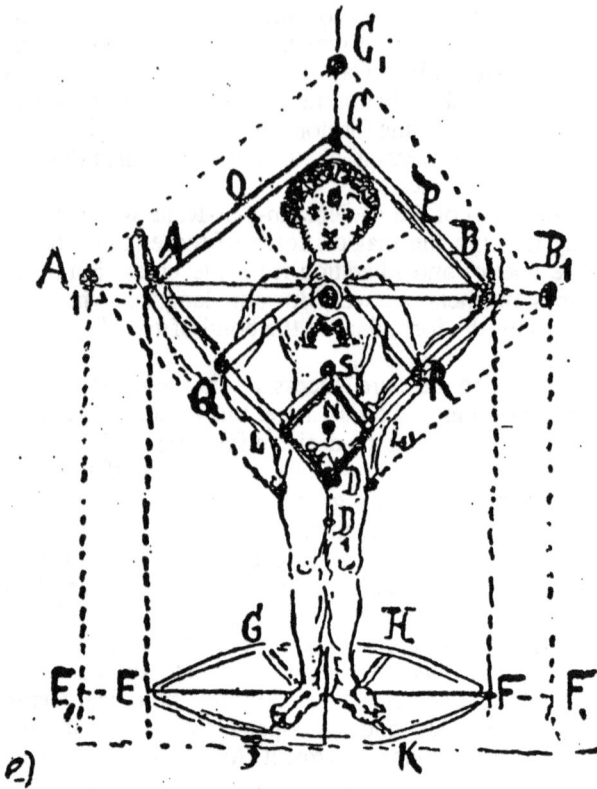

Figure 10e
The *Tabernaculum Hermetis* (the Armanic Tabernacle), in which all the Runes are contained as vibratory symbols of the Hermes-Brotherhood

## Conclusion

To be suspended on the cosmic antenna-apparatus is at first felt as suffering by the individual. But then the antenna-motif (*Ant-*, *And-war*) is transformed into Need!

In this book we saw the Need-motif as a key to the bond of all spiritual entities, through which all shall awaken to a new community, the World-Brotherhood of Spirits.

We showed how this awakening to this spiritual community is effected and how Wuotan-Mercury shows the way to this end, first to his own peopl, and ultimately to all of humanity.

His descent in the Ninth Night is a process which has to be experienced and elevated to the purpose of a universal religion. That God which is awakening on the Need-Rune is the Divine Ego, which is once more shaken awake by Need. But he is more. He is Mercury, the emissary from heaven, who, by releasing the cosmic Od-current in humanity now begins to raise up humanity into the next level of evolution and existence.

Here Christianity itself is brought to a close.

*Deus Odinus*, i.e. "within the Od dwells God" and therefore within the cloud in which he appears is the Parousia(21)!

So the Germanic peoples saw the Christian phenomenon in a deeper way, saw it *esoterically*, before it had ever been manifested *dogmatic-*

*ally*, indeed, before it ever entered into history! They experienced in "Wuotan of the Ninth Night" the revival of Christ on the cross and therefore too that of the Christian peoples after their Fall and their crucifixion by the Material-Spirit, *And-var*. They showed mankind the way.

By founding Esot-Congregations everywhere an effort should be made to advance the understanding of biblical Christianity.(22)

The *Edda* and the Aryan Kabbalah which lies at its root, as well as esoteric Buddhism and Brahmanism can also be of the highest service in this endeavor. The Bible and Christianity are dead today, but this is only because Christ has been killed a second time. May he be once more revived a second time in the Ninth Night!

The posture of the Svastika-sign as the key to the Hermes-Brotherhood. It contains the doubled Victory-Rune [*Sieg-Rune*]:

Sal— and Sieg (Salvation and Victory)!
in the greeting of the ancient Armanen (Hermionen).

# Appendix

f   u   th   o   r   k   h   n   i   a   s   t   b   l   y

**The runic tent** which contains all the Runes as symbols of engagement. Here the antenna-cross is shifted to the *coronarium*, C.

Runes are hieroglyphic-mathematical symbols of a universal spiritual language and represent vibrations of the Tat-æther, which permeates all systems.

The N- or Need-Rune, fundamental to these vibrations, was described in this book. Out of it are unfolded all the others in both name and kind. They open the gate of the "Tabernacle of the Arman" or the eternal tabernacle in which dwells the immortal man.

The names of the main Runes are: Feh, Ur, Thor, Os, Reid, Kaun, Hegl, Nôt, Is, Aar, Sig, Tyr, Biörk, Lögr, Yr.(23)

Meaningfully translated into our present-day language the names of the Runes signify powers by means of which the antenna-cross is caused to vibrate.

# Notes

1. The German word *Not* denotes several nuances which have to be taken into account when attempting to understand fully what is connoted by the use of the word "Need" in this translation. *Not* means "need, want, distress, misery; necessity, emergency, trouble, urgency, difficulty, danger." The cognate of this word, Old Norse *nauð* and Old English *nied*, constitute the name of the **n**-rune.

2. *Nysta* is the Old Norse preterite from the verb *nysa*, 'to pry, peer.'

3. From Nietzsche's *Also sprach Zarathustra*, Part One, "Von der schenkenden Tugend."

4. The so-called "High Song" of the *Edda* indicated here is the "Rúnatals þattr Óðins" which is identical to Hávamál (stanzas 138-165) in the *Poetic Edda*.

5. The Old Norse text has been improved slightly from that given by Shou, but the German translation has been rendered faithfully.

6. This is a reference to the Eddic verse found in "Sigrdrífumál" 8 which refers to carving the *nauð*-rune on one's nails.

7. These verses are taken from the "Hávamál" 140-141. Again the Old Norse text has been improved, leaving some irregularities important to Shou's translation, which has been rendered faithful to the original German.

8. This reference is to the conclusion of the work *Parsifal*, not the *Ring des Nibelungen*

9. Karl Vogt, Jacob Moleschott and Ludwig Büchner were the so-called classical triumvirate of 19th century German chemistry.

10. Andvara is the genitive form of the name Andvari, which is the Old Norse name of the dwarf in the *Volsunga Saga* (ch. 14) from whom the gods take the Nibelung treasure.

11. In fact the stem of *regin* has more to do with "advising."

12. The German words spelled *Acht* or *acht* allow for a wide range of nuances. These have to be taken into account when translating the word *Acht* in the original text. Sometimes it must be left untranslated. It can be the plural of the numeral eight used as a noun. More usually it denotes a "secret" or "underground tribunal."

13. This film was a serial originally shown in eight parts in 1919-20. It had various directors and was based on a novel by Karl Figdor (= Kurt Friedrich) published by Müller, Berlin, 1920.

14. I.e. the constellation of Cygnus

15. Vali and Vidar are sons of Odin in the *Eddas*, who avenge the deaths of Baldur and Odin respectively and who are specifically said to survive Ragnarök.

16. Named for Ernst Florens Friedrich Chlandni (1756-1827).

17. *Jedai'ah* which in Hebrew means literally "praise Jehovah," is a group of ancient Hebrew priests mentioned in I Chronicles 24:7 and Ezra 2:36 and Nehemiah 7:39 where they are seen as priests who survive the Babylonian captivity to return to Jerusalem. As a curious aside, the name was clearly used by George Lucas in the *Star Wars* films to create a name for his order of "Jedi Knights."

18. Shou's etymology of the word *muspell-* is a fanciful one. Controversy exists over whether this word is to be interpreted from a

traditional, heathen, perspective (in which case it would mean "spoiling of the earth") or from a Christian perspective (in which case it would mean "damnation by the spoken word [of God]). Its obscure and difficult formulations speaks to it most likely being an extremely archaic, and hence pre-Christian word and concept.

19. In the *Armanen* tradition the r-rune was sometimes called the rîta-rune, more usually the rit-rune. Rîta is a play on the Sanskrit word for right cosmic order, usually rendered *ŗta* or *rita*.

20. Here Shou again demonstrates his sympathies with the ideas of Marxism and the Russian Revolution of 1917 and its stated ideals as he tires to connect the Russian Bolsheviks with "*Bol-sh'wa*-Congregation."

21. *Parousia* is a Greek word for "presence." In Platonism this refers to the presence of an Idea in a thing of which is itself a reflection of the higher Idea. In Christian theology this term was used to denote the presence of Christ after his prophesied "second coming."

22. By "biblical" Shou means to imply *primitive*, or *original* Christianity, as taught by Jesus and which can be understood by esoterically decoding biblical texts.

23. These rune-names are not the Armanic ones used by Guido von List, but rather are irregular versions of the Younger Futhark names.

9 781885 972590